ELOHIM
JEHOVAH
ADONAI
JEHOVAH NISSI
JEHOVAH TSABA
JEHOVAH ROHI
JEHOV
EL ELYO
EL SHA
JESUS
IMMAN

THE **POWER** OF GOD'S NAMES

THE CREATOR GOD
THE RELATIONAL GOD
THE GOD WHO RULES
THE LORD MY BANNER
THE LORD OUR WARRIOR
THE LORD MY SHEPHERD
THE LORD OUR PROVIDER
THE MOST HIGH GOD
LORD GOD ALMIGHTY
THE GOD WHO SAVES
GOD WITH US

BEST-SELLING AUTHOR
TONY EVANS

LifeWay Press°; Nashville, Tennessee

ISBN 978-1-5359-7722-7 • Item 005819105

Dewey decimal classification: 231
Subject headings: GOD \ NAMES \ CHRISTIAN LIFE

Unless indicated otherwise, Scripture quotations are taken from the New American Standard Bible®, Copyright © 1960, 1962, 1963, 1968, 1971, 1972, 1973, 1975, 1977, 1995 by The Lockman Foundation. Used by permission. (www.lockman.org) Scripture quotations marked NIV are taken from the Holy Bible, NEW INTERNATIONAL VERSION®. Copyright © 1973, 1978, 1984 by Biblica Inc. All rights reserved worldwide. Used by permission. Scripture quotations marked HCSB are taken from the Holman Christian Standard Bible®, Copyright © 1999, 2000, 2002, 2003, 2009 by Holman Bible Publishers. Used by permission. Holman Christian Standard Bible® and HCSB® are federally registered trademarks of Holman Bible Publishers. Scripture quotations marked KJV are taken from the King James Version.

To order additional copies of this resource, write to LifeWay Resources Customer Service; One LifeWay Plaza; Nashville, TN 37234; phone toll free 800-458-2772; order online at LifeWay.com; fax 615-251-5933; email orderentry@lifeway.com; or visit the LifeWay Christian Store serving you.

Printed in the United States of America

Groups Ministry Publishing • LifeWay Resources
One LifeWay Plaza • Nashville, TN 37234

CONTENTS

ABOUT THE AUTHOR

Dr. Tony Evans is one of America's most respected leaders in evangelical circles. He's a pastor, a best-selling author, and a frequent speaker at Bible conferences and seminars throughout the nation. He has served as the senior pastor of Oak Cliff Bible Fellowship for more than forty years, witnessing its growth from ten people in 1976 to more than ten thousand congregants with more than one hundred ministries.

Dr. Evans also serves as the president of The Urban Alternative, a national ministry that seeks to restore hope and transform lives through the proclamation and application of God's Word. His daily radio broadcast, *The Alternative with Dr. Tony Evans,* can be heard on more than 1,300 radio outlets throughout the United States and in more than 130 countries.

Dr. Evans holds the honor of writing and publishing the first full-Bible commentary and study Bible by an African-American. A former chaplain for the Dallas Cowboys, he's currently the chaplain for the NBA's Dallas Mavericks, a team he has served for more than thirty years.

Through his local church and national ministry, Dr. Evans has set in motion a kingdom-agenda philosophy of ministry that teaches God's comprehensive rule over every area of life, as demonstrated through the individual, family, church, and society.

Dr. Evans is married to Lois, his wife and ministry partner of more than forty years. They are the proud parents of four—Chrystal, Priscilla, Anthony Jr., and Jonathan—and have a number of grandchildren.

CHAPTER 1

THE MAJESTY OF GOD'S NAMES

INTRODUCTION What's in a Name?

I'm sure you'll agree with me that names are important. Names are useful because they allow us to label and remember the different people, places, and things we encounter each day. Names are also significant because they give us starting points for understanding and inter-acting with the world around us.

For example, if I mention the city of Philadelphia, you may remember from history lessons in school that its name actu-ally means the city of brotherly love. When I talk about the city of Jerusalem, Bible scholars know its name means the city of peace. Even something as large and diverse as a city can be connected to a simple idea through the meaning of its name.

If you've been to Philly or Jerusalem lately or even if you watch the news every once in a while, you understand that the current culture and climate of those cities don't always match up with their names. Even so, the names are still important because they reveal how far those cities have moved away from the original intentions of the people who founded them.

Names are important. Names carry weight and meaning. But I need to make it clear at the beginning of our journey together that this isn't a study about names in general. It's not even a study about God's names—not primarily.

This is a study about God. Our goal is to increase our knowledge of God and to deepen our experiences with Him. We'll use His names as an entry point to achieve that goal, but always keep in mind that God's names are signifi-cant solely because they're connected to Him.

As we get started this week, we'll see that God's names carry a weight and majesty that far exceed any other name. And we'll begin our focus on God by exploring Him as Elohim—God, our strong Creator.

DAY 1 Introducing God's Names

Do you like your name? I like mine. Over the course of my life, different people have referred to me by a number of different names—Anthony, Tony, Mr. Evans, Dr. Evans, Pastor Evans, and more—but I've generally been happy with most of them. I'm comfortable with my name because it fits me comfortably.

That's not the case with everyone. In fact, I can remember that when I was young, some classmates always hated the first day of school. That's because the first day of school usually meant new teachers, and new teachers almost always used the official names recorded in their systems. The teacher would call out something like "Edward Robinson, are you present?" Then the kid would shoot his hand up and say, "I'm here, but please call me Eddie!"

How do you feel about your name? Why?

In what ways have those feelings changed throughout different seasons of your life?

Why Study God's Names?

Throughout this study we're going to explore God's names in several different ways and from several different angles. But I want to acknowledge at the beginning that someone reading this study may be skeptical about such an exploration. That person may wonder, *Why do we need to study the names of God? Is that really important?* There are two main reasons the answer to that question is yes.

First, it's important for us to study and learn about God's names because we're connected with those names as followers of Jesus. I'm a Christian. I'm inextricably linked to Christ and His name because of my status as a child of God. The same is true for anyone who considers himself to be a follower of Christ—including you. As we explore the majesty and power of God's names, we'll more deeply appreciate the privilege of being known for all eternity as followers of Christ.

How would you summarize our culture's understanding of and reaction to the name of Jesus?

How does our culture understand and react to the term Christian?

Second, it's also important for us to explore God's names because they provide opportunities to learn more about God Himself. More importantly, experiencing the wonder and power of God's names allows us to experience God more deeply.

That's really the heart of this study. I hope and pray as we take this journey to explore the names of God and all the wonderful things they reveal, we'll experience His presence in a real and meaningful way. Let that be your goal in the weeks to come.

Why So Many Names?

God has many names. We've already mentioned two common ways we refer to Him in our culture today—Jesus and Christ—but that's just scratching the surface. In fact, there's no way we could do justice in this study to even half of God's names recorded in the Bible.

For that reason I'll focus our study on some of the primary names God used to reveal Himself in Scripture—names like Elohim, Jehovah, Adonai, El Shaddai, Immanuel, and more. These will serve as a helpful introduction to God's majestic, multidimensional name.

What are the major names and titles you use to address God or speak about Him?

How do you decide which name to use in different situations?

Maybe you're curious about the large number of God's names represented in Scripture. Maybe you're wondering, *Why does God have so many names in the first place? Why can't we know Him simply as God?*

One reason God gave us so many names to refer to Him is so that we can gain a better perspective on who He is. In other words, the reason we need so many names is that one name by itself doesn't fully describe God's majesty and power. One name alone can't fully communicate all of who He is.

You can see this principle at work in the way our culture responds to superstar athletes. When an individual rises above the rest and becomes truly great, we typically respond by giving him a nickname. That's how a defensive tackle in the NFL named Charles Edward Greene became Mean Joe Greene. He was too good for just one name. That's how Wayne Gretzky became The Great One in the National Hockey League. And that's why you rarely hear about a basketball player named Julius Erving; you hear about Dr. J instead.

We use multiple names to highlight the unique attributes of people we consider great. It's appropriate, then, that God uses multiple names to communicate His many attributes and the majesty of His greatness to us.

What attributes of God are most meaningful to you? Why?

In over four decades of ministry and six decades of life, I've become increasingly convinced that God desires for us to know Him for all He truly is. As we understand and experience the many aspects of His goodness and power, our hearts are opened to worshiping Him.

God wants us to come face-to-face with the many layers of His significance and identity. His names reveal various facets of His character. In fact, throughout the Bible, when God wanted to reveal a new part of His character to His people, He often did so by revealing a new name.

That's what happened with Moses in his encounter with God at the burning bush:

> Moses said to God, "Behold, I am going to the sons of Israel, and I will say to them, 'The God of your fathers has sent me to you.' Now they may say to me, 'What is His name?' What shall I say to them?" God said to Moses, "I AM WHO I AM"; and He said, "Thus you shall say to the sons of Israel, 'I AM has sent me to you.'"
>
> **EXODUS 3:13-14**

What does the name I AM teach us about God and His attributes?

Moses knew he couldn't take command of the Israelites and lead them out of Egypt based on his own name and his own authority. That's why he needed to know God's name. Moses needed to connect himself to a specific attribute of God in order to display the power attached to God's name.

God responded to Moses by revealing one of my favorite names in Scripture: "I AM WHO I AM" (v. 14). We'll go deeper into the meaning and power of this name later in the study. For now simply understand that God told Moses all he needed to know about Himself for Moses to respond in obedience, and He did it by revealing His name.

Be prepared for a similar experience this week as we begin this journey toward a more meaningful experience with God and a deeper understanding of the power of His names.

DAY 2 The Majesty of God's Name

The ability to name a child is one of the greatest privileges exercised by parents—and one of the greatest responsibilities. Names are significant, and I believe parents should make the most of the opportunity by blessing their children with names that mean something, not just names that sound cool.

You may have noticed that some parents name their children after celebrities or other influential people. For example, in recent decades many parents have named their sons Michael Jordan in hopes of forging a connection between their child and Jordan's athletic ability. Others have named their kids after Beyoncé or other famous people in an attempt to emulate their favorite celebrity. I've even had people from Africa send me photos of their children named Tony Evans!

What are some of your favorite names? Why?

What do you know about the origins or history of your name?

Of course, being named after a person doesn't mean you actually receive any talents or abilities from that person. A person who's been named Michael Jordan can be entirely clumsy and uncoordinated. The name alone contains no special power without the character and abilities to support it. Nomenclature doesn't equate with substance.

Remember that today as we explore the majesty of God's name. His name is indeed great but only because it receives its substance from Him.

How Majestic Is God's Name

The beginning of Psalm 8 is one of the most popular and most frequently quoted verses in all Scripture about the splendor of God's name:

> O LORD, our Lord,
> How majestic is Your name in all the earth,
> Who have displayed Your
> splendor above the heavens!
> **PSALM 8:1**

The names of God reflect the majesty and glory that intrinsically rest within Him. His name is nothing short of pure majesty. Discovering and experiencing the manifestation of His names in your life will usher you directly into the presence of our majestic God. That's what this study is all about.

What ideas or images come to mind when you hear the word *majesty*?

My wife and I recently took a trip to Alaska with several hundred partners and ministry supporters of our radio ministry, The Urban Alternative. Alaska is one of our favorite places to visit, simply because of its relaxing nature and inspiring beauty. Yet something special happened on this trip. Our cruise guide, who had hosted well over 90 cruises in the same area, told us he'd never seen the weather so perfect. Each day the skies were clear and beautiful, giving us many opportunities to marvel at the splendor of God's creation.

In fact, things were so perfect that our guide named that trip the atheist cruise. He said, "If someone was an atheist when they got on this cruise, they couldn't be by the time it was over."

When have you been most impressed or awed by the majesty of the natural world?

This is the kind of majesty David wrote about in Psalm 8. Like my wife and me, David had been awed by the splendor of God's creation. He responded by recognizing his own smallness and insignificance in comparison to the majesty of God's name expressed through creation:

> *When I consider Your heavens,*
> *the work of Your fingers,*
> *The moon and the stars, which*
> *You have ordained;*
> *What is man that You take thought of him,*
> *And the son of man that You care for him?*
> **PSALM 8:3-4**

Maybe you've picked up this study and already believe you have it all together, resting in the reality of your success and achievements. If so, you may be able to pronounce God's names by the time you flip over the last page, but you won't experience the power of His names in your life. Not if you've got an inflated sense of your own worth.

How would you honestly rate your sense of self-worth and importance?

1   2   3   4   5   6   7   8   9   10
I recognize my smallness.   **I feel very important.**

What elements of modern culture encourage us to inflate our own sense of worth and importance?

The majesty of God is reserved for those who know enough to know they don't know much of anything at all. In other words, you can't know the splendor of God's names until you come to grips with the smallness of your own.

What experiences cause you to recognize the majesty of God?

Hallowed Be God's Name

Jesus' words at the beginning of the Lord's Prayer also address the importance of God's name:

> *Our Father who is in heaven,*
> *Hallowed be Your name.*
> **MATTHEW 6:9**

The term *hallowed* comes from the Greek word we typically translate as *holy*. It means to *be set apart* or *sanctified*. In other words, God's names are unique. They're not for us to mix up with anyone else's name or to treat lightly. God's names are hallowed. They're to be honored, respected, and treated with the reverence they deserve.

For example, if the president of the United States walked into the room, you wouldn't address him in an informal way. You wouldn't say, "What's up, Dude?" The position of president demands a certain degree of recognition and respect.

Who are some of the people you respect most in the world? Record at least three.

1.

2.

3.

In what ways does your manner of speaking with these people differ from your manner of speaking with everyone else?

Obviously, God's names are to be treated with even higher respect than what we'd give to any person on earth. We're commanded to hallow His names—not only the verbalization of His names but also the way we think about and reflect on them.

To hallow God's names means to treat them as if they carry weight—as if they're significant. It means we recognize that God isn't an ordinary Being and that His names aren't ordinary names. We're not flippant about them. Certainly we shouldn't take His names in vain, as we'll see tomorrow. But we can also hallow God's names simply by choosing to use them only in a way that communicates reverence, respect, worship, and even fear.

To know God's names is to experience His nature, and that level of intimacy is reserved for those who are humbly dependent on Him. Because God doesn't share His glory with another (see Isa. 42:8), we must humble ourselves if we really want to know Him. We must recognize our own insignificance before we can experience the significance that comes only through Him.

What steps have you taken to honor and revere God's name?

God's name is majestic. It's unique and set apart—something worthy of being hallowed through our actions and attitudes. Only when we hallow God's name can we hope to truly experience its power.

Conclude your study today by contemplating the majesty and holiness of God. Then speak with Him about it. Use His names with reverence and awe as you praise His majesty.

DAY 3 Taking God's Name in Vain

People who grew up in my generation were generally familiar with the Ten Commandments. Even people who didn't go to church could name most of them. And if you attended church in those days, as most people did, you were especially familiar with the Third Commandment:

> *You shall not take the name of the LORD your God in vain, for the LORD will not leave him unpunished who takes His name in vain.*
> **EXODUS 20:7**

We usually heard the commandments in the King James Version back then:

> *Thou shalt not take the name of the LORD thy God in vain; for the LORD will not hold him guiltless that taketh his name in vain.*
> **EXODUS 20:7, KJV**

For my generation this was a rock-solid command. Saying anything that could be interpreted as taking God's name in vain would most likely get your mouth washed out with soap. It was serious business.

How would you define what it means to take God's name in vain?

Where in our culture do you see God's name being taken in vain?

As we get ready to explore specific examples of God's names, let's first make sure we understand exactly what it means to take His name in vain. We also need to understand the consequences of making that unwise decision.

A Lack of Substance

The word we translate as *vain* in Exodus 20:7 literally means *empty* or *without meaning*. It conveys the idea that something is without substance. Therefore, taking God's name in vain has to do with using God's name in a way that isn't consistent with the substance of His person and the weight of His character. It's the opposite of hallowing His name.

In short, to take God's name in vain is to strip away the value that belongs with God's name because it's connected to Him.

What emotions do you experience when you hear other people take God's name in vain? Why?

What situations tempt you to use God's name in vain?

Sadly, taking God's name in vain is a common occurrence in the world today. Many people joke about God's name and toss it around flippantly. Worse, they fire it off in anger and use it as a curse. These are common examples of what it traditionally means to take God's name in vain.

But taking God's name in vain goes to a deeper level, one that can apply even to Christians if we're not careful. This happens when we attempt to define God or speak on His behalf in a way that's contrary to His character. Too many people in our culture attempt to define God based on their own personal desires. They try to make Him say whatever they want so that they can do whatever they want.

Why is it tempting to use God's name to support our opinions?

A blatant example of using God's name in vain occurred in the garden of Eden. You know the story. Satan wanted to tempt Adam and Eve into disobeying God, and he started with these words:

The serpent was more crafty than any beast of the field which the LORD God had made. And he said to the woman, "Indeed, has God said, 'You shall not eat from any tree of the garden'?"

GENESIS 3:1

Notice the Devil didn't have any problem bringing up God's name. In fact, he knew he wouldn't get very far with Adam or Eve if he left God out of the discussion. So he invoked God's name in a way that supported his own desires and advanced his own agenda. He used God's name in vain.

In Genesis 2 God was referred to as the LORD God in relation to humanity, which is a combination of two names: Jehovah and Elohim. Elohim, the name of God used in Genesis 1, points to God as Creator, while Jehovah points to His relational authority over humankind. In the creation narrative those two terms combine to paint a powerful portrait of God as both the powerful Creator of the universe and the personal Lord over His creation.

When Satan mentioned God, however, he used only the name Elohim. He dropped the name that spoke of God's relational authority over people because he wanted to define God on his own terms.

What are some modern examples of people using God's name to advance their own purposes?

What steps can you take to avoid abusing God's name in those ways?

Abusing God's name goes beyond cursing like a sailor or uttering phrases like "Oh my God." Too many of us want a God we can easily understand—a God to neatly display on a bumper sticker or on a coffee mug. But the true God won't be confined. His names reflect His character, and He wants a genuine love relationship with His children, not an empty relationship in which people use His names for their own purposes.

A Lack of Fear

One reason so many people in our culture choose to take God's name in vain is that our culture as a whole has lost the fear of His name. We no longer respect God's position and power, so we no longer honor His name. We don't approach His name with the respect it deserves.

This is a mistake. Why? Because fearing God's name is a primary catalyst for living a life that's pleasing to Him. That's what David learned:

> *Teach me Your way, O LORD;*
> *I will walk in Your truth;*
> *Unite my heart to fear Your name.*
> **PSALM 86:11**

Read Psalm 86:11-17. What do these verses teach about God and His name?

To fear God and His name can mean to be afraid of Him—to realize His awesome power in contrast with your weakness. Fearing God can also mean living with a reverence for and awe of who He is. In both cases fearing God's name ushers in the ability to walk in God's way and in His truth. It's the key to living an abundant life and to fulfilling your destiny as a member of God's kingdom.

Which activities in your daily routine help you fear God and respect His name?

Over and over in Scripture God showed up in people's lives in miraculous ways. And if we look closely at what He's revealed about the various aspects of His character through the manifestation of His names, we'll respond appropriately. We'll fear, revere, and worship Him because of His greatness and power.

In a similar way, if you pay attention to what God has done in your life, you'll fear Him. You'll give Him praise. Did He wake you up this morning? Has He supplied all your needs? Has He put food on your table, kept you safe, and healed your body? Even if you've suffered and experienced trials, hasn't He offered you the fullness of His presence and His peace when you've humbled yourself before Him? Hasn't He promised to be with you and never to forsake you?

For all these reasons and more, we're to honor and fear God's great name. And in honoring, knowing, and experiencing His name, we find power not only to face life's circumstances but also to rise far above them in the abundance of His mercy and grace.

In what ways have you recently experienced God's power and provision?

As we begin our study of God's names, be prepared to discover God in ways you've never imagined and to know and experience Him more deeply through His powerful, majestic names.

DAY 4 Introducing Elohim

You've probably heard the saying "You never get a second chance to make a first impression." It's true. First impressions leave lasting impressions. That's why we usually try to put our best foot forward when we meet people for the first time.

That's another reason names are so important. They're an integral part of any first impression.

What techniques do you typically use when trying to make a good first impression?

God doesn't need to make good first impressions, of course. He's God! He always acts consistently with His character, and any person who has a genuine encounter with Him always comes away impressed.

Still, it's interesting to note that the first verse of the Bible basically serves as God's introduction to humanity:

> *In the beginning God created the*
> *heavens and the earth.*
> **GENESIS 1:1**

What are your impressions of God, based on this verse?

The name God used to describe Himself in Genesis 1:1 is Elohim, which means strong Creator God. Of all the different names for God in the Bible, He chose Elohim to be the first. This was His introduction. This was the first impression He offered to His creation.

In essence God said, "Hello. I'm Elohim." Let's explore the implications of that choice for those of us who follow God today.

Elohim Is Transcendent

Why did God choose for us to get to know Him first and foremost as Elohim, the Creator God? One primary reason could be that He wanted us to recognize the transcendent quality of His nature and character.

Maybe you haven't heard God described that way before. *Transcendent* is a big theological word that means God is distinct from everything He created. God isn't categorized within His creation. He's not a tree, a river, a butterfly, or anything else that exists as part of creation. God is lifted above and outside it all. He's transcendent.

Interestingly, the apostle Paul noted in Romans 1 that the existence of creation itself serves as evidence pointing to Someone who exists outside creation. In other words, the existence of creation itself points to the reality of a Creator:

Since the creation of the world His invisible attributes, His eternal power and divine nature, have been clearly seen, being understood through what has been made, so that they are without excuse.

ROMANS 1:20

Why is it important for us to understand God's transcendent nature?

Another reason God introduced Himself as Elohim is that it distinguishes Him as being set apart from the constraints of time. When we read, "In the beginning God created ..." (Gen. 1:1), we discern that God created the beginning. He created time as we know it. And if God created time, then He preceded time, because you can't create time unless you first exist before time.

In other words, God is eternal. While we as human beings are forced to deal with the problem of time and its many consequences in our lives, the same isn't true of God. He transcends time.

Read the following passages of Scripture and record how they contribute to your understanding of God's eternal nature.

Isaiah 44:6-8

Revelation 1:8

21

Not only does Elohim transcend creation and time, but He also transcends space. Everything you and I know and experience is contained within the heavens and the earth. Even with a tool as powerful as the Hubble telescope, we can perceive only what exists in our physical universe. We can't comprehend anything beyond the heavens and the earth because that's the space in which we exist; it's where we've been placed.

Yet God existed when space didn't. He created the physical world we know as the heavens and the earth, so He exists outside that physical world. He transcends creation, time, space, matter, and anything else we can comprehend.

Elohim Is Immanent

Look at this description of God from the Book of Jeremiah:

> *"Am I a God who is near," declares the LORD,*
> *"And not a God far off?*
> *Can a man hide himself in hiding places*
> *So I do not see him?" declares the LORD.*
> *"Do I not fill the heavens and the*
> *   earth?" declares the LORD.*
>
> **JEREMIAH 23:23-24**

These verses give us a glimpse into the delicate balance of God's presence, and I choose the word *balance* intentionally. In this passage God proclaimed Himself to be both transcendent *and* immanent. Elohim created the heavens and the earth, existing outside it. Yet that word *immanent* means Elohim also fills the heavens and the earth, existing within it. He is here, there, and everywhere!

At the same time, we shouldn't think of our Creator God as an energy source like the force in *Star Wars*. Elohim isn't a "May the force be with you" Being. In fact, as we continue reading Genesis 1, we discover very different attributes of God connected with His name Elohim:

> *[Elohim] said, "Let there be an expanse in the midst*
> *of the waters, and let it separate the waters from the*

waters." [Elohim] made the expanse, and separated
the waters which were below the expanse from the
waters which were above the expanse; and it was
so. [Elohim] called the expanse heaven. And there
was evening and there was morning, a second day.

GENESIS 1:6-8

What do these verses communicate about God's nature?

Look at the action words in those verses: "God said." "God made." "God called." Our Creator isn't merely a spirit floating around in never-never land. While He's other-dimensional and beyond our comprehension, He's also intensely involved with His creation. In fact, if we skim a few chapters forward in the Genesis account, we find Him walking and talking with Adam and Eve in the cool of the day (see Gen. 3:8).

Why is it important for us to recognize the fact that God wants to be intimately engaged with His creation?

This aspect of God's nature is good news for us because it helps us understand that we don't live in an impersonal universe, nor do we serve an impersonal God. It's true that Elohim is transcendent and beyond our comprehension. But it's also true that He manifests Himself within creation and reveals Himself to us in ways we can understand.

The best news of all is that Elohim, the strong Creator, involves Himself in the lives of human beings as the crown of His creation. That includes you.

As you pray throughout the day, make a conscious effort to speak with God not as a creative force but as a Person who wants to be involved in your life. Talk with Him about your thoughts, fears, and desires. Thank Him for wanting to be engaged in your life.

DAY 5 Elohim: The Strong Creator

We're exploring the power of God's names, so I think it's appropriate that we've started with Elohim, the strong Creator God.

Yesterday we noted that God used the name Elohim to introduce Himself to humanity in Genesis 1. We also explored reasons God chose to use that name as a first impression: because the name Elohim points both to God's transcendence over all creation and to His personal interaction with creation.

In short, the name Elohim affirms right at the beginning of Scripture that God chooses to balance His extreme power and His intimate concern in relating to you and me.

How have you experienced God's power in your life?

How have you experienced God's personal care in your specific circumstances?

Today we'll conclude our study of the name Elohim by considering practical implications for our lives as we experience God's power and personal involvement.

Responding to God's Power

In the early pages of Scripture, God identified Himself as Elohim 35 times. In fact, Elohim is the only name used for God in Genesis 1:1–2:3. One reason I believe God placed this focus on Elohim at the beginning of His Word is that He wanted to display His power. The literal translation of the name Elohim means Strong One in the Hebrew language. The name communicates both God's sovereignty and His authority, and it reflects His ability to accomplish anything He desires.

How do you see God's power at work in the world today?

In addition, the way Elohim is used in the opening chapters of Genesis points directly to God as Creator. We began exploring that connection yesterday, but here's an additional truth I don't want you to miss: the Hebrew term translated *created* is used only in connection with God throughout the Bible. Human beings are never the subject of a sentence in which *created* is the verb.

The reason is that people are not creators. People can reconfigure, recalibrate, redesign, or reform things that have been created, but no human beings can create something totally on their own. We lack the power, ingenuity, and ability to create anything *ex nihilo*—out of nothing—as God does.

God's creative power is reinforced throughout the Bible, including this passage from the Book of Hebrews:

> *By faith we understand that the worlds were prepared by the word of God, so that what is seen was not made out of things which are visible.*
> **HEBREWS 11:3**

How does this verse reflect God's power as Creator?

Why is faith necessary to connect with God as Creator?

So what does God's identity as strong Creator God mean for you? How can you connect with Elohim's power as you live, work, and seek to serve Him each day?

I want to encourage you to remember the name Elohim whenever you face challenges or difficult circumstances in your life. Remember that your strong Creator God doesn't need any raw materials in order to work. He doesn't need logic or tangible solutions to accomplish His plan for you each day. All He needs is Himself, and all you need is faith in His name—faith that He can do all He purposes to do.

What circumstances in your life feel beyond your control?

How do you typically respond when life gets difficult? What actions do you take?

Too often we get hung up on trying to see a solution when circumstances are difficult and life gets hard. That's human nature. Even as Christians, we try to create solutions to our problems instead of turning to God. Even when we call on Him, we often suggest creative ways for Him to straighten out our situation, tweak our trial, or fix our failure.

What we need to do is remember God's name, because Elohim is more than able to create something out of nothing in our lives. He's done it before, and He can do it for you and me if we call on His name and then get out of the way.

Responding to God's Involvement

So far we've considered the name Elohim in connection with Genesis 1:1. Yet something very interesting and relevant for our everyday lives happened in verse 2:

> *The earth was formless and void, and darkness was over the surface of the deep, and the Spirit of God was moving over the surface of the waters.*
>
> **GENESIS 1:2**

The Hebrew term translated *formless and void* is *tohu wa-bohu*. It refers to a physical location that's uninhabitable, almost to the point of being a wasteland. But that wasn't the end of the story. Elohim was present in the midst of that wasteland, and He cared enough to hover over the chaos and create life.

If we fast-forward to Genesis 3, we see another mess that was created, this time due to the impact of sin:

> *The LORD God called to the man, and said to him, "Where are you?" He said, "I heard the sound of You in the garden, and I was afraid because I was naked; so I hid myself." And He said, "Who told you that you were naked? Have you eaten from the tree of which I commanded you not to eat?" The man said, "The woman whom You gave to be with me, she gave me from the tree, and I ate." Then the LORD God said to the woman, "What is this you have done?" And the woman said, "The serpent deceived me, and I ate."*
>
> **GENESIS 3:9-13**

What's your initial reaction to these verses? Why?

Talk about a mess. God had created a paradise for Adam and Eve, one that was supposed to extend to all humanity throughout history. But this paradise was ruined by the corruption of sin. It became another wasteland.

How have you seen the impact of sin in the world today?

Yet all hope wasn't lost, because Elohim was there. Elohim, who had hovered over *tohu wa-bohu* and created life, also had the power to redeem His creation from the corruption of sin. Just as important, Elohim cared enough about His creation to step into the mess and die on a cross in order to make us clean. That's the message of the gospel.

Therefore, one of the greatest lessons to learn about God, about Elohim, is He can not only create from nothing, but He can also take something the Devil has junked up

THE POWER OF GOD'S NAMES

and fix it. He can make it right again. And He *will* make it right again because He cares. He's just that involved in our world and our lives.

When Satan attempts to bring mess into your life and produce death where there once was life, God's Spirit has the ability to turn what Satan has destroyed into something beautiful again. He can make something dead live again. Elohim is a God who transforms a mess into a miracle. He transforms darkness into light. He transforms the desolate, uninhabitable recesses of your soul into places of fertile growth.

Read Psalm 139. What are some ways God knows you intimately?

What steps can you take to remember and rely on Elohim's power and personal care for you?

When times are tough and you don't know how to solve the problems bearing down on you, remember Elohim. Remember that He can make something from nothing and let it flourish into something grand, even when it looks as if nothing is happening at all. He cares enough about His creation to bring order out of chaos—even in your life and mine. His is a great name because He's a great and powerful God.

Think about the area of your life you identified as being out of control. Have you presented it to Elohim and asked Him to create something new and beautiful from it? If not, do that now. Then spend time praising Him for His power and intimate care for you.

CHAPTER 2

JEHOVAH & ADONAI

INTRODUCTION Pieces of the Puzzle

One day a little boy was drawing a picture in art class at school. The teacher walked over and asked him, "What are you drawing?"

Without a moment's hesitation the boy said, "I'm drawing a picture of God."

"A picture of God?" she replied. "You can't draw a picture of God. No one knows what God looks like."

Just as quickly the boy replied, "They will when I'm done."

Everyone has their own view of what God is like. As Christians, we have the opportunity to study the ways God has revealed Himself through His Word. We can know Him personally, and we can know a lot about Him. But as flawed and finite human beings, none of us are capable of understanding everything about God. As a result, none of us have a completely accurate picture of God.

The good news is that as we continue our study of the power of God's names, we'll expand our knowledge of God. Each name we encounter is like another piece in the puzzle of God's nature and character. Of course, that's a puzzle we'll never finish because God is far beyond our comprehension. But the more pieces we gather, the more we'll grow in our understanding of who God is and what it means to serve Him.

With that in mind, let's familiarize ourselves this week with Jehovah and Adonai—two vital pieces of the puzzle made up of God's names.

DAY 1 Introducing Jehovah

Branding has become a popular buzzword in business circles today. On an intellectual level, branding involves the conceptual formation of perspectives that reach beyond mere nomenclature and into the heart and identity of what's been branded. To put the idea in layman's terms, branding involves the way consumers emotionally react to a specific company or product.

I like what David D'Allesandro wrote in his book *Brand Warfare:*

> *By definition, "brand" is whatever the consumer thinks of when he or she hears your company's name. Thanks to the information revolution, "whatever" now includes labor practices, quality controls, environmental record, customer service, and every rumor that wings its way around the Internet.*[1]

For example, if I say the name Ford, you'll automatically have some kind of reaction to that brand, based on your past perceptions and experiences. The same is true for any major company—Apple, McDonald's, General Electric, and so on. Because these companies want to sell products to you, they invest a lot of effort and energy in establishing a positive connection between you and their company names. That's what branding is all about.

We're studying the power of God's names. Interestingly, as we get to know God's names in Scripture, we also learn that God's names have been branded. His names aren't merely words. Rather, each name carries a specific weight, substance, and meaning. God's names matter, and we'll be able to connect with God on a deeper level as we get to know the various "brand promises" connected with each name.

Last week we focused on Elohim, which depicts God as our strong Creator. Today we'll continue our exploration of God's names by focusing on the name used most often throughout Scripture—more than six thousand times in the Old Testament alone. In many ways, it's God's most famous name.

It's the name Jehovah, meaning Self-Existing One or Self-Revealing One. Interestingly, Jehovah is the English translation of the Hebrew name for God, which is YHWH, or Yahweh. So Jehovah and Yahweh are actually the same name.

An Encounter with Jehovah

To best understand the meaning of the name Jehovah, we need to take a look at the life of Moses. In the Book of Exodus we find Moses at a time in his life when he was struggling with his purpose.

Read Exodus 2:11-15. What strikes you as most interesting in this account?

How would you describe Moses' position in life at the end of these verses?

Moses had grown up as a man with great promise and potential in Egypt. However, he lost his life of privilege by murdering an Egyptian soldier in an attempt to defend his people, the Hebrews. This act caused even his own people to fear him and turn against him. Rejected by both people groups and afraid for his life because of Pharaoh's retribution, Moses fled to the wilderness and took a job shepherding sheep.

Moses was a shepherd for 40 years in the desert of Midian, and it's safe to say his former potential had withered to a crisp. He'd once been a confident leader, but now his life held very little value, even in his own eyes. That's when God showed up:

Moses was pasturing the flock of Jethro his father-in-law, the priest of Midian; and he led the flock to the west side of the wilderness and came to Horeb, the mountain of God. The angel of the LORD appeared to him in a blazing fire from the midst of a bush; and he looked, and behold, the bush was burning with fire, yet the bush was not consumed. So Moses said, "I must turn aside now and

see this marvelous sight, why the bush is not burned up."
EXODUS 3:1-3

What do these verses teach us about Moses and his character?

Talk about an interruption in your day! After 40 years in the desert, Moses had no doubt become accustomed to the same old landscape, the same old sheep, and the same old routine. But the burning bush changed all that. God was about to confront Moses with the challenge of a lifetime, while revealing Himself in a way Moses hadn't experienced before.

Between a Rock and a Hard Place

Have you ever been stuck between a rock and a hard place? I have. Throughout my life I've found myself in several circumstances in which it seemed every option was a bad option and every choice led to an undesirable consequence. Call them what we like—stuck between a rock and a hard place, up a creek without a paddle, out on a limb, and so on—these are the kinds of situations that test our resolve on many different levels.

When have you found yourself between a rock and a hard place?

How do you typically respond when you find yourself in difficult situations?

Most of the time we get ourselves into rock-and-a-hard-place situations. We get backed into a corner with no good way out because we chose to ignore the warning signs flashing in front of our faces. Most of the time.

But you need to understand that God sometimes allows us—or even pushes us—into situations that seem to have no solution. Why? Because He wants us to understand that *He's* the solution. Sometimes God lets us hit rock bottom because He wants us to realize that *He's* the Rock at the bottom.

The good news is that God usually brings us into these negative or confusing situations when He wants to reveal something new about Himself. That's what He did with Moses:

> *When the LORD saw that he turned aside to look,*
> *God called to him from the midst of the bush and*
> *said, "Moses, Moses!" And he said, "Here I am."*
> **EXODUS 3:4**

When has God captured your attention through strange or difficult circumstances?

Notice in the text that God—Jehovah—didn't reveal Himself to Moses until Moses turned aside from his ordinary routine. When God wants to show you a new dimension of Himself you've never encountered before, He often uses something that doesn't make sense. He often reveals Himself through a mess, a problem, a confusing situation—something like a burning bush. God uses these situations to capture our attention from our humdrum, earthbound pursuits.

When you find yourself in confusing or painful circumstances, don't focus all your attention on the confusion or pain. And don't focus on business as usual. Why? Because you might miss God. When you allow the circumstances of life to consume all your energy and all your attention, you run the risk of missing something important that God wants you to see, experience, or understand. You run the risk of missing God. So when you confront a mess in life, stay focused on Him so that you'll be ready to receive what He wants to show you.

What are some obstacles in today's culture that often prevent people from missing God's revelation of His character?

What steps can you take to actively focus on God in the midst of difficult or confusing circumstances?

Take it from me: you don't want to miss God when He wants to reveal Himself in your life.

DAY 2 Mission Impossible

In the 1960s television show "Mission Impossible," each episode started with agent Jim Phelps receiving a message on a recording that said, "Good morning, Mr. Phelps." He was then given details of a situation with instructions that began, "Your mission, should you choose to accept it ..." It usually involved a dangerous situation that required him and his team to place their lives on the line. The recording always ended like this: "As always, should you or any of your IM force be caught or killed, the secretary will disavow any knowledge of your actions. Good luck, Jim. This tape will self-destruct in five seconds."

In the desert of Midian, Moses received his "Mission Impossible" assignment. As you know, Moses encountered God when he turned aside to see the burning bush. Moses came into God's presence, and God spoke with him. God ultimately charged Moses to return to Egypt; confront Pharaoh; and lead God's people, the Israelites, out of slavery and into a life of blessing in the promised land (see Ex. 3:5-10).

Moses immediately realized this was a task too great for him:

> *Moses said to God, "Who am I, that I should go to Pharaoh, and that I should bring the sons of Israel out of Egypt?"*
> **EXODUS 3:11**

God assured Moses that He would be with him and gave him a sign:

*He said, "Certainly I will be with you, and this
shall be the sign to you that it is I who have sent
you: when you have brought the people out of
Egypt, you shall worship God at this mountain."*
EXODUS 3:12

When Moses thought about everything God promised and
everything God commanded him to accomplish, he balked.
He was afraid. Moses knew Pharaoh wanted to kill him, and
he didn't know how the Israelites would respond when they
saw him again.

So Moses asked God a question. It reads this way in
my Tony Evans translation: "When I go down to Egypt and
meet up with all these folk who don't like me, who should
I say sent me to talk with them?" In other words, "God,
what name should I give to Pharaoh and to Your people as
evidence that You've sent me?"

Here's how God answered:

*God said to Moses, "I AM WHO I AM"; and He said,
"Thus you shall say to the sons of Israel, 'I AM
has sent me to you.' " God, furthermore, said to
Moses, "Thus you shall say to the sons of Israel,
'The LORD, the God of your fathers, the God of
Abraham, the God of Isaac, and the God of Jacob,
has sent me to you.' This is My name forever, and
this is My memorial-name to all generations."*
EXODUS 3:14-16

**How do these verses contribute to your understanding
of God?**

This is Jehovah, "I AM WHO I AM" (v. 14). As I said earlier,
this is the name most commonly used for God in the Old
Testament. But the main reason this name is so important
is that it's the way God told Moses—and by extension His
people, the Israelites—who He is.

Implications of the Name Jehovah

I don't want you to miss the importance of that name Jehovah—I AM WHO I AM. The name reveals several important facts about God's nature and character.

1. THE NAME JEHOVAH TELLS US THAT GOD IS SELF-GENERATING AND SELF-EXISTING.

As human beings, all of us present on planet Earth are alive because we were created. We were preceded by a mother and a father. We *are* because they *were*. Thus, every person alive today can say, "I am." But none of us can say, "I am who I am." We don't exist within ourselves or by our own power.

That isn't the case for Jehovah. He isn't dependent on anyone or anything else for His existence. He exists totally within Himself. Nothing outside God caused Him to be created, nor does anything contribute to or maintain His essence. He's entirely self-sufficient, dependent only on Himself. He's I AM WHO I AM.

Why is it important for us to understand that God exists entirely at His own initiative and by His own power?

2. ANOTHER IMPLICATION OF THE NAME JEHOVAH IS THAT GOD IS *IMMUTABLE,* WHICH IS A FANCY WORD THAT MEANS HE DOESN'T CHANGE.

God's always the same. He's in the eternal present tense. On a practical level, this means God can never become irrelevant; He's always current. A billion years from now, God will still be just as relevant as He was on the day He spoke the universe into existence, because the entirety of creation will still be dependent on Him. You can't get much more relevant than that!

3. A FINAL IMPLICATION OF THE NAME JEHOVAH IS THAT GOD WILL ALWAYS BE WHO HE IS.

He will always be I AM WHO I AM, which means He won't necessarily be who we *want* Him to be. God exists within Himself. We have zero ability to define Him or shove Him into a box of our choosing.

When have you been tempted to define God based on who you wanted Him to be?

What steps can you take to consciously approach God based on His character rather than on your desires?

When you approach God on the basis of who He says He is, you're ready to see Him as I AM WHO I AM—Jehovah, the Relational God. And you don't want to miss Jehovah. He offers a relationship that's both powerful and deeply personal.

Don't Be Afraid to Get Personal

So far in this study we've explored two critically important names of God: Elohim and Jehovah. Elohim is God's creative and powerful name, while Jehovah is God's personal name. Jehovah is His self-revealing name, because God directly gave it in response to Moses' question "What's Your name?"

Essentially, when we study the name Elohim, we study God as the Creator. We're talking about His power, presence, and prowess. But when we talk about Jehovah, we're talking about God's more personal side—His personal character. Elohim connects with the aspect of God that created the heavens and the earth. Jehovah connects with the aspect of God that personally relates to His creation.

I find it interesting to study the transition between these two names in the early chapters of Genesis. In Genesis 1:1–2:3 we see God as Elohim forming His creation. In Genesis 2:4 the text introduces a new name—Jehovah. This is where we begin to see God interacting with creation in a new way.

Instead of simply creating, Jehovah became personally involved with the well-being and purpose of what He'd made.

In fact, just as we saw Jehovah interacting with Moses and calling him in Exodus 3, we see Him interacting with humankind in Genesis 2. The LORD (Jehovah) God—

- "formed man" (v. 7);
- "planted a garden" (v. 8);
- "caused to grow" (v. 9);
- "took the man and put him into the garden" (v. 15);
- "commanded the man" (v. 16);
- "formed every beast … and brought them to the man" (v. 19);
- "caused a deep sleep to fall upon the man" (v. 21);
- "took one of his ribs and closed up the flesh" (v. 21);
- "fashioned into a woman the rib which He had taken" (v. 22).

All these descriptions point to God's personal involvement with His creation. So we must never be afraid to respond personally to our Creator. In fact, such a response is necessary if we want to experience a relationship with Jehovah.

It's entirely possible for people to believe in God as Elohim without knowing Jehovah. In fact, plenty of people today believe in God; they believe in the existence of Elohim, the Creator. Yet many of these same people have no direct, personal knowledge of God. They don't know God as Jehovah.

Why do some people prefer an impersonal Creator to a personal God who knows us and wants us to know Him?

I know Jehovah is an Old Testament name, one we don't often come across today except in a few hymns. But we must recognize God as Jehovah—as the God who reveals Himself to us—if we want to experience a personal relationship with Him. In fact, we must understand God as Jehovah if we want to follow Christ.

In fact, Jesus Himself referred to the name Jehovah— I AM WHO I AM—in describing Himself:

*Jesus said to them, "Truly, truly, I say to you,
before Abraham was born, **I am.**" Therefore
they picked up stones to throw at Him, but
Jesus hid Himself and went out of the temple.*

JOHN 8:58-59, EMPHASIS ADDED

What do these verses teach us about Jesus?

The Pharisees and religious leaders of Jesus' day were often obstinate, but they weren't dummies. When they asked Jesus who He thought He was, and He replied by saying, "I am" (v. 58), the war was on. They knew He was declaring Himself to be God.

To understand God as Jehovah is to understand that He's a Person. He's I AM, and He wants to know us personally.

In what ways do you need the personal touch of Jehovah today?

DAY 3 Knowing Jehovah

When I was growing up, there were basically two ways to get to know another person: talking on the phone or talking face-to-face. That was it. If you wanted to make a connection with someone, you either called them on the telephone—which wasn't always easy since phones had wires and were connected to the wall back then—or you sat down with them to have a chat.

Things are different today. If you want to get to know another person, you can still call them or talk with them face-to-face. But now you've got other options.

For example, you can make a connection through social media to get a good idea of their style and personality, including what they like and dislike. Or you can read their blog or visit their website to study their opinions on different issues. You can instantaneously engage them in written conversations through email or texts. You can even talk with them from the comfort of your home by using video-conferencing software.

So we've got a variety of options today. What I'm still trying to figure out is whether those options are helping or hindering our efforts to connect with the people we care about!

What are your favorite ways to connect with other people? Why?

What are some of the pros and cons of using technology to communicate with others?

We've been studying Jehovah, the name of God that reveals His personal nature and personal connection with His creation. Jehovah is I AM WHO I AM, the changeless, self-sufficient LORD over the universe. Yet Jehovah also demonstrates a desire to interact with the universe, including you and me, in an intimate way.

So that begs an important question. How do we get to know God as Jehovah? Let's explore two answers to that question.

Ask for Jehovah

In Exodus 33 we get a vivid picture of the incredible relationship Moses enjoyed with God:

Moses used to take the tent and pitch it outside the camp, a good distance from the camp, and he called it the tent of meeting. Whenever Moses entered the tent, the pillar of cloud would descend and stand at the entrance of the tent; and the LORD would speak with Moses. When all the people saw the pillar of cloud standing at the entrance of the tent, all the people would arise and worship, each at the entrance of his tent. Thus the LORD used to speak to Moses face to face, just as a man speaks to his friend.

EXODUS 33:7,9-11

What strikes you as most interesting about these verses?

That last verse blows my mind: God talked with Moses "face to face, just as a man speaks to his friend" (v. 11). That's incredible. Other than Adam and Eve, no one else in the Old Testament enjoyed such an intimate relationship with Jehovah God.

How did that relationship come about? We don't know all the details, but we get an interesting clue later in the same chapter: "Moses said, 'I pray You, show me Your glory!' " (v. 18).

One reason Moses was able to develop such a close relationship with God was that he asked for it, plain and simple. And the reason Moses asked for a deeper relationship with God was that he truly *desired* a deeper relationship with God. He *wanted* to know God. Moses sought God with a passion because he was passionate about connecting with Him.

How would you honestly rate your desire to know God on a deeper level?

1	2	3	4	5	6	7	8	9	10

No desire   **Strong desire**

What steps have you taken in the past to deepen your relationship with God?

When little children wanted to meet Jesus, they and their parents asked to see Him (see Mark 10:13-15). When Mary wanted to know Jesus more deeply, she forgot everything else and sat at His feet (see Luke 10:39). Sometimes we make things more complicated than they need to be. If we want to know God more intimately, we simply need to seek Him with all our hearts.

Always Ask for More

Let's circle back to Moses' request of God: "I pray You, show me Your glory!" (Ex. 33:18). Although Moses had come face-to-face with Jehovah God, he still wanted more. He asked to see more of God—to know more. And God granted his request:

> *He said, "I Myself will make all My goodness pass*
> *before you, and will proclaim the name of the LORD*
> *before you; and I will be gracious to whom I will*
> *be gracious, and will show compassion on whom*
> *I will show compassion." But He said, "You cannot*
> *see My face, for no man can see Me and live!"*
>
> **EXODUS 33:19-20**

When have you seen visible evidence of God's goodness and grace?

What's fascinating to me about this whole situation is that Moses could have been satisfied with the burning bush (see Ex. 3). He could have been satisfied with the 10 miraculous plagues (see Ex. 7:14–11:10). He could have been more than satisfied with the parting of the Red Sea and the destruction of Pharaoh's armies (see Ex. 14:21-31). But Moses wasn't satisfied. He wanted more of God. And more. And even more.

Do you know why so many of us don't know Jehovah and don't experience Him more personally in our daily lives? It's because we're too busy and too distracted to ask for more.

What's your response to the previous statement?

Too many Christians today stop at the burning bush. We're satisfied with an introduction to God's power. Yet as we've seen, Jehovah is the relational, intimate God. He will come as close to us as possible if we ask Him and seek Him as Moses did.

Moses made the effort and took the time to be in the presence of Jehovah and say to Him, "LORD, I want to know You more. Show me more of You." If Moses were alive today, he'd have turned off the television and the radio. He'd have stopped texting and phoning his friends so that He could seek time with God. He would've spent less time at the do-it-yourself shops or the ballgames.

In other words, Moses removed the static from the line and the noise from all around him, clearing away the distractions so that he could enter God's presence in the tent of meeting and ask to see Him. If we want to see God at work in our lives, we need to do what Moses did.

What obstacles prevent you from spending more time in God's presence?

What steps can you take to remove some of those obstacles and allow time to ask God for more of Himself?

Many Christians today say they want to know more of God. But when you take a closer look at their lives, you see they're just talking noise. Jehovah knows when we're just spouting words and when we truly desire to get closer to Him. And He will respond accordingly.

Moses had dedicated the time and effort before he ever requested to see God. For that reason God gave Moses something no other human on the planet was experiencing: the personal, manifest presence of His glory.

If you desire to know Jehovah, ask for Him. Seek Him and spend time in His presence. The rewards are far greater than you can imagine.

Spend time worshiping Jehovah—the self-existent, all-sufficient God. Express your desire to know Him personally and to see Him meet all your needs. Ask Him to make Himself known to you and to work powerfully in your life.

DAY 4 Introducing Adonai

Since we're studying God's names, I'd like to tell you about a little trick you can use to distinguish between some of those names as you read your Bible. You've probably noticed that most Bibles use a number of English terms when referring to God. Sometimes a Bible verse refers to God, other times to the Father, other times to the Mighty One of Jacob, and so on.

Lord is another English term commonly used in reference to God. But if you look closely at your Bible, you'll see that the word *Lord* isn't always printed the same way. Sometimes the text uses small capitals: LORD. On other occasions the text uses Lord, with only the *L* being capitalized.

You can see examples of both terms in this passage:

> *After these things the word of the **LORD** came to*
> *Abram in a vision, saying,*
> *"Do not fear, Abram,*
> *I am a shield to you;*
> *Your reward shall be very great."*
> *Abram said, "O **Lord** GOD, what will You*
> *give me, since I am childless, and the heir*
> *of my house is Eliezer of Damascus?"*
> **GENESIS 15:1-2, EMPHASIS ADDED**

Here's the trick. Whenever you see the word *LORD* in all capitals, it refers to the name Jehovah (Yahweh). Whenever you see *Lord,* it refers to the next name in our study: Adonai, the Lord and Master.

**How has your growing awareness of God's names
affected your interactions with His Word?**

**What are some other tools you can use to identify the
names of God when you study the Bible?**

The Importance of Ownership

Like Elohim, Adonai is a plural name. In the Bible it occurs in the plural form because God is a plural Person. He's only one God, but He's made up of a plurality: the Father, the Son, and the Holy Spirit.

The name Adonai, found more than four hundred times in the Bible, is full of meaning. The cultural background of the word *adon* is associated with masters who owned

44

slaves. Yet the term didn't merely connote ownership; it also bore a certain responsibility for the care and well-being of what was owned. The master was to provide for, protect, guide, and maximize what he owned.

What responsibilities are associated with ownership in our culture today?

So when Scripture refers to God as Adonai, He's identified as Owner. The psalmist wrote that God is "the [Adonai] of the whole earth" (Ps. 97:5). He's not only the Creator (Elohim) but also the Owner (Adonai). God's ownership of creation is proclaimed throughout His Word, including here:

> *Every beast of the forest is Mine,*
> *The cattle on a thousand hills.*
> *I know every bird of the mountains,*
> *And everything that moves*
> *in the field is Mine.*
> *If I were hungry I would not tell you,*
> *For the world is Mine, and all it contains.*
> **PSALM 50:10-12**

Why is it important for us to understand that God is the Owner of all creation?

What are the implications of God's ownership of your life and property?

In the New Testament the apostles often called themselves the bond servants or bond slaves of Jesus Christ (for example, see Rom. 1:1; Jas. 1:1; Jude 1). By intentionally using this language, the disciples were letting everyone know their status as individuals owned by Christ—by Adonai.

The Importance of Submission

Sometimes the implications of acknowledging God as Adonai can make people feel uncomfortable. Why? Because if we say God is the Owner of all creation, that includes us! If we recognize God as Adonai, as the Owner of all things, then we must submit to His ownership.

What's your response to the previous statements?

Moses understood the importance of submission in this context. As we've seen, he was more than a little unsure of himself during his conversation with God after the burning bush. In fact, Moses balked when God showed up after four decades and offered him the commission of a lifetime.

Even so, look at the way Moses addressed God throughout the conversation:

> *Moses said to the LORD [Jehovah], "Please, Lord [Adonai], I have never been eloquent, neither recently nor in time past, nor since You have spoken to Your servant; for I am slow of speech and slow of tongue."*
> **EXODUS 4:10**

God responded by reminding Moses of His power: "Who has made man's mouth? ... Is it not I, the LORD [Jehovah]?" (v. 11). Then Moses replied again: "Please, Lord [Adonai], now send the message by whomever You will" (v. 13).

What can we learn from Moses' choice of names when he addressed God?

It's true that Moses doubted his abilities; he may have also doubted God's calling on his life. But even in the midst of that doubt, Moses still recognized that God was in charge. Moreover, he recognized that God *owned* him; he made his plea to Adonai, the Owner and Master of all things.

In other words, Moses may not have understood the potential of God's power in his life, but at least he understood who runs the show.

Too many people want to access God's power without giving Him the right to own them. The truth is that God isn't going to give you more of Jehovah by revealing Himself and His ways to you if you're not willing to confess Him as Adonai—if you're not willing to surrender ownership of your time, thoughts, talents, and treasures to Him.

One problem in the body of Christ is that too many Christians want God to get them to heaven, but they don't want God to own them on earth. But unless there's an Adonai confession of God, then your Jehovah experience of His self-revelation will be limited. You may hear His Word—you may even say, "God's promises are true; amen"—yet the fulfillment of those promises in your life are often tied to your level of surrender to Him as Adonai.

In what areas have you resisted God's ownership of your life?

What steps can you take to let go of those areas and surrender them to Him?

Businesspeople would never invest heavily in something over which they had no access or ownership. The same is true of God. He must have the right to own you if He's going to take the responsibility of doing something with your life.

DAY 5 Surrendering to Adonai

Most leadership positions in the world today aren't available to just anyone. You typically have to qualify, based on specific requirements. For example, to be elected president of the United States, you must be at least 35 years old, a natural-born citizen of the United States, and a U.S. resident for at least 14 years.

Of course, a potential president must also secure the primary nomination of his political party and triumph at the end of a grueling political campaign, but you get the idea. Certain positions require specific qualifications to be filled effectively.

What are some positions or tasks in today's society for which you're specifically qualified?

What roles or tasks are you qualified to undertake in God's kingdom?

You may feel you're not qualified to do the things God's called you to do. That's understandable. That's a common feeling. But remember God has the power to make you qualified. That's what he did with Moses. And that's what he did with the man we're going to focus on today—Gideon.

A Paltry Pedigree

We first meet Gideon at a time when his people, the Israelites, were being pounded by the Midianites. The Midianites were a pagan people, yet they were oppressing the Israelites because God's chosen people were dabbling with false gods and worshiping idols. Therefore, God allowed the enemy to take over.

Eventually, the Israelites got tired of the situation and cried out to God. Having been made low by the Midianite oppression (see Judg. 6:6), they recognized their desperation. They rightly turned back to God for relief and deliverance.

When God heard their cry, He came down and had a talk with Gideon.

Read Judges 6:11-18. What are your initial impressions of Gideon?

When in your life have you felt that God wasn't holding up His end of the bargain?

Just as He had with Moses, God presented Gideon with an amazing call: to "deliver Israel from the hand of Midian" (v. 14). But just like Moses, Gideon balked. He allowed doubt and fear to hold him back.

Even so, look at the language Gideon used when addressing God:

> *O Lord [Adonai], how shall I deliver Israel?*
> *Behold, my family is the least in Manasseh,*
> *and I am the youngest in my father's house.*
> **JUDGES 6:15**

Gideon had a paltry pedigree. And yet, just like Moses, Gideon didn't allow his fear to prevent him from addressing God as Adonai—as the Owner of all things, including himself. Even as he focused too much on his own weakness, Gideon still recognized God's authority. Of course, Gideon went on to defeat the Midianites in God's name and with His power (see 7:19-23).

When have you accomplished something that can be explained only by God's power at work in you?

I love Gideon's story because it powerfully illustrates God's ability to use any of us, no matter what our background is or which side of the tracks we come from. God can use us to accomplish His purposes even when we don't feel confident in our abilities—even when we possess shortcomings that present legitimate obstacles to our success.

When we consider Gideon's story, we can make a connection between the Midianites and the various strongholds that keep people oppressed, addicted, or defeated today. Whether it's a chemical addiction, negative influences, poor self-esteem, or people who are trying to prevent you from living out your purpose, God makes it clear that when He's your Adonai, you'll see Him work things out as your Jehovah. He will reveal paths and plans to you, and it's likely those plans will include strategies you never would have thought of on your own.

What strongholds or obstacles are currently holding you back from fulfilling your calling and God-given purpose?

Acknowledgment Versus Surrender

Scripture tells us that each of us came into this world with nothing and that we'll all leave this world with nothing. Everything you have is on loan. You merely borrow God's resources. In fact, the Bible says if you're a believer and a follower of Jesus Christ, even your body isn't your own:

> *Do you not know that your body is a temple of the Holy Spirit who is in you, whom you have from God, and that you are not your own? For you have been bought with a price: therefore glorify God in your body.*
>
> **1 CORINTHIANS 6:19-20**

Unless God completely owns you, you'll be limited in how much of Him you experience. Sure, you may hear a lot about Him in His Word—you may hear a lot of sermons and read a lot of Christian material—but your experience of God is entirely tied to your recognition that He's Adonai, your Master and Lord.

To what degree have you surrendered your life and resources to God's ownership?

1	2	3	4	5	6	7	8	9	10

Not surrendered   **Fully surrendered**

What steps can you take to approach God as Adonai and more fully surrender control of your life to Him?

I'm not yet a huge fan of computers; I don't use any. But I have an iPad, so I'm aware that sometimes you need a password to get to different features on your iPad, such as email, apps, and so on. Spiritually speaking, surrendering to God as Adonai is the password for unveiling Jehovah in your life. It's the password to God's expressing, revealing, and manifesting Himself in your situation.

To approach God as Adonai requires obedience and sacrifice. Calling on God as Adonai moves you toward a heart that's set on following what He says because it recognizes Him as the Owner; therefore, He calls the shots. Jesus framed it this way:

> *Why do you call Me, "Lord, Lord,"*
> *and do not do what I say?"*
> **LUKE 6:46**

What does it mean to you when you think of Jesus as Lord?

There's nothing to fear in surrendering to God as your Owner. Imagine that Bill Gates comes up to you and says, "If you let me own your finances, I'll take care of you financially." Would you feel afraid? It's doubtful anyone would argue with that proposition. After all, Bill Gates is a master at financial stewardship and prosperity. Your knowledge of him would lead you to trust his owning that arena of your life.

Similarly, your knowledge of God—through His names and His character—ought to give you the freedom to fully surrender to His care as your Owner. He's got you covered. He possesses all you need. He has your best interest at heart. He just wants you to confess Him as Adonai, as Master and Lord.

Spend time today confessing God as Adonai, the Owner of your life and of all you possess. Acknowledge any areas of your life you haven't fully surrendered to Him and ask Him to help you do so. Ask Him to use your abilities and gifts to carry out what He's called you to do. Surrender to Him as your Lord and Master.

1. David D'Allesandro, *Brand Warfare: 10 Rules for Building the Killer Brand* (New York: McGraw-Hill, 2001), xiv.

CHAPTER 3

JEHOVAH NISSI & JEHOVAH TSABA

INTRODUCTION Jehovah Fights for You

Experience has convinced me that many of the fights taking place in the world today are frivolous. They're unnecessary. Individuals fight over sinful desires or wounded pride. Nations fight over limited resources or a desire for power. What does it all gain?

When we look back over history, however, it quickly becomes clear that some fights achieve important goals in the world. Some battles need to be fought.

Take the Battle of Gettysburg, for example, widely considered a primary turning point in the American Civil War. Under the leadership of Robert E. Lee, the Confederate army had been pushing northward in an attempt to shift the battleground of the conflict. Many historians believe Lee intended to invade all the way to Philadelphia and beyond. He was ready to go for the throat of his enemies and end the war for good.

The Northern forces, commanded by General George Meade, were tired and poorly provisioned. They were desperate for a victory—something they could use to turn the tide and secure momentum in order to move forward.

The battle lasted for three days in July 1863. Each day the Confederate soldiers charged, attempting to break the Union lines. Each day the Northern armies held. When it was over, almost 50,000 soldiers had lost their lives on both sides—a terrible loss. And yet the battle helped preserve freedom for millions of individuals and created a brighter future for our nation and the world.

Some things are worth fighting for. And as we'll see this week, nothing is better than having God fight for us in those

situations. He's Jehovah Nissi, the LORD My Banner. And
He's Jehovah Tsaba, the LORD Our Warrior.

Through the power of His names, we can have victory.

DAY 1 Introducing Jehovah Nissi

When we say we want to get to know God, we're usually
talking about getting to know one of His character qualities.
We want to learn something new about Him. We want Him to
reveal Himself to us in a new way.

**How has this study helped you experience God in
a new way?**

God revealed new information about Himself several times
in Scripture. Typically, He did so by tying the name Jehovah
to another name that revealed His character on a deeper
level. For example, when Gideon became terrified after
speaking with God and was convinced he was about to die,
God told him to be at peace. After encountering something
new about God that day, Gideon built an altar to Jehovah
Shalom—"The LORD is peace" (Judg. 6:24).

We do the same thing in today's culture with celebrities
and public figures. When athletes distinguish themselves
through a specific trait or skill, we give them a secondary
name that highlights that characteristic. For example, base-
ball player Hank Aaron was known as Hammerin' Hank,
a title that was driven home when he passed Babe Ruth's
record of 714 home runs in a career.

**What are some other popular compound names in
today's culture?**

I use the phrase *compound connection* when referring to God's
compound names. I like these names for two main reasons.

1. They occurred at important moments in Scripture when God unveiled Himself and offered a new revelation of His character.
2. Compound connections typically occurred at a particularly challenging moment in the life of a person or a group of people. God gave these names during times of need.

Both of those reasons were evident when God revealed the name we'll study today—Jehovah Nissi.

An Unwanted Fight

When we look at the Israelites in Exodus 17, we encounter a group of people who felt greatly discouraged. We know this because of the amount of complaining they were doing. The Israelites had been rescued from slavery in Egypt, yet they launched a firestorm of grumbling when they realized "there was no water for the people to drink" (v. 1).

Read Exodus 17:1-7. How would you summarize the complaints of the Israelites?

Whenever I read that account, I'm struck by this verse:

> [Moses] named the place Massah and
> Meribah because of the quarrel of the sons
> of Israel, and because they tested the LORD,
> saying, "Is the LORD among us, or not?"
>
> **EXODUS 17:7**

It's easy for us to judge the Israelites as we read their accusatory question against God. But I imagine we've all asked that question at some point: "Is the LORD among us or not?" We've all had moments when we thought, *Where is God? Why can't I ever find Him when I need Him the most?*

When have you recently asked those kinds of questions?

54

What specific situations typically cause you to question God?

The Israelites were tired, hungry, and thirsty, so they questioned whether God cared for them and whether He was still interested in their situation. And that's when they suffered an unwanted attack: "Amalek came and fought against Israel at Rephidim" (v. 8).

Isn't life like that sometimes? Whenever we feel we've hit rock bottom, someone throws us a shovel and tells us to dig a little deeper. Fortunately for Moses and the Israelites, God *was* still among them. In fact, they were about to experience the power and provision of Jehovah Nissi—the LORD My Banner.

An Unconventional Victory

When the Amalekites attacked, Moses knew it wasn't a situation from which the Israelites could run or retreat. Although they were tired and worn down, they needed to face the situation head on if they had any hope of survival. So Moses gave instructions to Joshua, his military commander:

> *Choose men for us and go out, fight against Amalek. Tomorrow I will station myself on the top of the hill with the staff of God in my hand.*
> **EXODUS 17:9**

That's exactly what happened. Moses climbed to the top of a nearby hill, while Joshua and the Israelite army engaged the Amalekites in the valley below. Interestingly, the text tells us that whenever Moses raised his staff high, the Israelite army prospered in the battle. But whenever his arms got tired and his staff started to fall, the Amalekites began to prevail.

This pattern indicated that the battle wasn't entirely physical. A supernatural element was involved in the fight, and it was connected to Moses' staff. And the reason Moses' staff was important was that God had sanctified it. This was the same staff that had turned into a snake (see Ex. 4:2-5), ushered in the plagues (see Ex. 7–10), brought water from a rock (see Ex. 17:5-6), and opened up the Red Sea (see Ex. 14:16). The staff had become a symbol through which God used natural things to perform supernatural works and to display His power.

What are some other symbols in Scripture that represent God's power and supernatural influence in the world?

Moses was involved in a spiritual battle on top of that hill, and spiritual battles are tiring. As Moses continued to hold the staff high, his "hands were heavy" (Ex. 17:12). He grew weary and began to lose strength. Fortunately, help was at hand. As Moses faded, Aaron and Hur stood beside him and held up his hands, ensuring a victory for God's people (see vv. 12-13).

Don't ever feel you have to face the trials of life on your own. In fact, don't ever think you're *able* to face the trials of life on your own—because you're not. You need help, and so do I. That's one reason I'm so thankful God created the church. It provides us a place to find Aarons and Hurs in our time of need.

Do you find it easy or difficult to ask for help? Explain.

How have you recently benefited from the support of fellow Christians and church members?

When the battle was over and the Israelites had come through victorious, Moses knew something important had happened. He understood that God had done something new, and he appropriately responded through worship:

> *Moses built an altar and named it The*
> *LORD is My Banner [Jehovah Nissi].*
> **EXODUS 17:15**

Today we usually associate a banner with a flag or a piece of material placed on display. But in biblical times a banner could refer to any number of items. In this case the banner was Moses' staff—what I like to think of as the rod of God.

To approach God as Jehovah Nissi is to look toward Him as the source of power and deliverance in your life. The LORD My Banner means God has made Himself evident and available for those who look to Him in times of need.

What steps can you take to access God's power and deliverance during your times of need?

It's true that most Christians today don't have experience with anything like the rod of God. We don't have physical banners that help us focus on God's presence and access His power. Yet, as we'll see tomorrow, God has still given us a banner to use each day as we deal with the realities and challenges of life.

DAY 2 Jesus Christ: Our Banner

I saw a movie several years ago that still reminds me of the principles connected with Jehovah Nissi, the LORD My Banner. That movie, *Inception,* is still one of my favorites. In the film the characters could enter dreams. In fact, they could enter a dream within a dream—or a dream within a dream within a dream. As you can imagine, the characters could easily become confused about what was real and what wasn't. So they used a physical item called a totem to determine whether they were experiencing a dream or a reality.

The main character's totem was a spinning top. When he spun the top, he knew he was in a dream if it kept spinning indefinitely. If it came to a stop, however, he was in the real world. This information was important because it informed him about what he could do. He could take much greater risks in a dream because the consequences weren't as severe; if something went wrong, he just woke up. The totem became his method for measuring reality and determining his plans.

The reason I like this illustration is that life can be confusing at times for all us. We all have moments when we don't know whether we're up or down, in or out. Therefore, we all need a standard outside ourselves to tell us what's real and what's not. We need something stable that can help us determine reality and make decisions. We need an objective standard that isn't connected to our emotions, thoughts, or desires.

That standard is Jesus. He's our Nissi, our Banner, in a chaotic, confusing world.

What motivated you to follow Jesus as Savior and Lord?

How has Jesus raised up the standard for your life in recent years?

Before we can fully appreciate Jesus as our Banner, we need to discover another important principle revealed by the Israelites' victory over the Amalekites in Exodus 17.

Seeking Balance

If you remember the account from yesterday, the Israelites' battle with the Amalekites was a strange combination of natural armies and supernatural intervention. On the one hand, Joshua and the Israelite soldiers had a role to play in fighting the Amalekites down in the valley. On the other hand, the outcome of the battle didn't depend solely on their efforts. The Israelites could achieve victory only as long as Moses, standing on a mountain overlooking the battle, was able to raise his staff into the air.

In other words, the battle was a mix of both physical and spiritual warfare.

What ideas or images come to mind when you hear the term *spiritual warfare*?

In my years of serving God in the church, I've noticed that people often respond with two extremes when they need to fight for something valuable—whether that means fighting for a marriage, a family, a child, health situations, or work situations.

Some people fight only from the mountain. They say, "I'm going to trust God and stay in touch with Him, and He will fix everything." Other people go to the opposite extreme of seeking to win the battle entirely in the valley. They look to their own skills, willpower, determination, and resources to overcome whatever they're facing, all the while neglecting God.

Which of these two extremes typically describes you? Explain.

The truth is in the middle. You must bring both the valley and the mountain together if you want to experience victory in your life. As a believer in Christ and a follower of God, you have a responsibility to do all you can to address the challenges and trials you face. Yet, unless God also supports and engages with you in the fight, your efforts won't be enough.

As Paul wrote:

> *He made Him who knew no sin to be sin on our behalf, so that we might become the righteousness of God in Him. And **working together with Him**, we also urge you not to receive the grace of God in vain.*
>
> **2 CORINTHIANS 5:21–6:1, EMPHASIS ADDED**

There are legitimate moments in life when God instructs us to wait. But there are also times when people say they're waiting on God to do something, yet He's actually waiting on them to walk by faith.

The key is to find a balance between what God does on the mountain and what we're responsible for in the valley. We're never to excuse irresponsibility in the name of God. Yet our personal responsibility alone isn't sufficient to achieve all He wants to accomplish in the midst of our conflicts, battles, and wars.

What battles are you fighting today?

What biblical principles or truths can help you find a balance between your responsibilities and God's power in difficult times?

Lifted Up

In Numbers 21 we find an interesting story that foreshadows Jesus' connection with Jehovah Nissi, the LORD My Banner. The Israelites had once again rebelled against God, so He sent poisonous snakes into their midst. Many of the Israelites died. It didn't matter where they went for help because they weren't facing a normal infestation. It was a spiritual consequence of their rebellion against God.

Eventually, the Israelites cried out to God for mercy, and He heard them. Look at what happened next:

> *The LORD said to Moses, "Make a fiery serpent, and set it on a standard; and it shall come about, that everyone who is bitten, when he looks at it, he will live." And Moses made a bronze serpent and set it on the standard; and it came about, that if a serpent bit any man, when he looked to the bronze serpent, he lived.*
>
> **NUMBERS 21:8-9**

What's your initial reaction to these verses? Why?

God didn't advocate idolatry or voodoo by commanding Moses to raise up the bronze serpent. Instead, God provided a banner of healing for the Israelite community. He identified a specific symbol that was set apart and sanctified—just like the rod of God we studied yesterday—so that the people could focus on it as a way to access God's power.

Now look at what the apostle John wrote hundreds of years later:

As Moses lifted up the serpent in the wilderness, even so must the Son of Man be lifted up; so that whoever believes will in Him have eternal life.

JOHN 3:14-15

How do you understand the term "lifted up" in verse 14?

How do these verses contribute to your understanding of Jesus and His work in the world?

Our Nissi today is Jesus Christ. He's our Banner, and whoever looks to Him will have access to God's supernatural power for salvation and eternal life.

And let me say this: Christ is our *only* Banner today. It doesn't matter how good you are, how much you try, how much money you earn, or how hard you work. All your good efforts will result in nothing if you don't look to the Banner of Christ for your eternal victory.

Read 2 Corinthians 2:14 and Colossians 2:15. What do these Scriptures teach you about Jesus as your Banner?

Before you give up, look up. Fix your eyes on Jesus, your Nissi. Your victory has already been won. Jesus will always enable you to triumph (see 2 Cor. 2:14) because He's already defeated Satan through His work on the cross (see Col. 2:15). That makes us more than conquerors, no matter what life brings our way.

Spend time today praying to Jehovah Nissi. Claim Jesus as your Banner and ask Him to fight for you in the battles you're facing.

DAY 3 Introducing Jehovah Tsaba

I turned 51 on September 10, 2001. It was a good day—an enjoyable day. I sometimes look back on that day with a strange kind of nostalgia because the next day, September 11, was one of the darkest days in our nation's history. Two airplanes crashed into the World Trade Center towers in New York. Another plane went down in a field, and another flew directly into the Pentagon.

What emotions do you experience when you reflect on the events of September 11?

How has your life been affected by those events?

Since September 11 the giant of terrorism has haunted and taunted our nation, including our most elite trained military personnel. It's a giant who battles according to a different set of rules. It doesn't discriminate. Its victims cross age, racial, economic, and gender lines. Terrorism is a brutal giant who seeks to rule through fear and intimidation and to destroy anyone in his way.

A lot changed after our nation met this giant. The fabric of our land was torn. And while we are in the courageous process of rebuilding and restoring what was lost, as well as continuing to defend what remains, many of us still demonstrate a lingering tendency to look over our shoulders. Giants are difficult to forget as well.

Why do I bring up such painful memories? Because our next name of God is found in a story about one of the most infamous giants in history—Goliath.

What ideas come to mind when you hear the name Goliath?

As we rehearse the details of the story, we'll highlight the power that can be released when we understand God's names.

The Giant

Described in 1 Samuel 17, the battle between David and Goliath is far and away the most famous representative battle in history. If you're not familiar with that term, representative battles involved two or more warriors who fought against each other in single combat. The winner of that fight imputed the larger victory to his entire army. Likewise, the loser imputed his defeat to the rest of his men.

Because the story of David versus Goliath has become so common, it's easy for us to lose the sheer vastness of Goliath as a physical specimen. According to the text, he was more than nine feet nine inches tall—tall enough to peek over the top of a basketball rim if he stood on his toes. Goliath was no string bean either. He was broad enough to wear "scale-armor which weighed five thousand shekels of bronze" (v. 5). That's almost two hundred pounds of armor on his upper body alone!

Read the entire description of Goliath in 1 Samuel 17:4-11. Which images or descriptions strike you as most impressive?

The backdrop of this story is a conflict between two people groups: the Israelites and the Philistines. Armies had gathered on opposing hills (see v. 3), with neither force willing to leave the high ground and launch a full attack on the enemy. However, the armies weren't idle—not the Philistine army, at least. Each day Goliath emerged from the ranks of the Philistines and threw down a challenge:

> *He stood and shouted to the ranks of Israel and said to them, "Why do you come out to draw up in battle array? Am I not the Philistine and you servants of Saul? Choose a man for yourselves and let him come down to me. If he is able to fight with me and kill me, then we will become your servants; but if I prevail against him and kill him, then you shall become our servants and serve*

us." Again the Philistine said, "I defy the ranks of Israel this day; give me a man that we may fight together."
1 SAMUEL 17:8-10

Most of us can handle the regular problems and normal challenges of life. We don't like them, but when they loom in the distance, we manage to keep going. But when a giant shows up in our lives—when we encounter something against which we have no hope of victory—that changes everything.

What are some of the giant problems people encounter in our culture today?

Has the fear of a giant ever gripped you to such a degree that it prevents you from moving forward? Maybe you've encountered such a giant on your job, in your home, or with your health. Whatever it is, the giant calls the shots, dictating your emotions and your actions or inaction. The giant sets the agenda, hoards the ball, and won't go away—just like Goliath.

What giant problems are you facing?

The Lord of Hosts

It was in the midst of the Israelites' fear and discouragement that David entered the scene. And it soon became clear that David viewed Goliath with a very different perspective than the rest of his people did:

David spoke to the men who were standing by him, saying, "What will be done for the man who kills this Philistine and takes away the reproach from Israel? For who is this uncircumcised Philistine, that he should taunt the armies of the living God?"
1 SAMUEL 17:26

Did you catch David's unique perspective on Goliath? The rest of the Israelites saw the same giant as David, but they didn't view that giant the same way. Everyone else looked at Goliath's size, strength, and armor. David zeroed in on a critical reality: Goliath hadn't been circumcised.

What images or sensations come to mind when you hear the word *circumcision*?

To be circumcised meant you belonged to the family of God. Therefore, to be uncircumcised meant you had no access to the power of God's names. That's the reality David focused on—not Goliath's physical size and strength but his spiritual weakness.

In other words, the rest of the Israelites looked at the situation and saw Goliath. David saw God.

Why is it so difficult to see beyond the physical and superficial aspects of our difficulties?

What steps can you take to focus on spiritual realities when you're facing a giant?

Goliath must have shared the same perspective as the Israelites, because when David showed up to accept his challenge, the giant thought the whole thing was a joke. He insulted David and cursed him by the Philistine gods.

David stayed cool. He maintained the proper perspective and delivered one of the greatest battle speeches in history:

You come to me with a sword, a spear, and a javelin, but I come to you in the name of the LORD of hosts [Jehovah Tsabal, the God of the armies of Israel, whom you have taunted. This day the LORD will deliver you up into my hands, and I will strike you down and remove your head from you. And I will give the dead bodies of the army of the Philistines this day to the

birds of the sky and the wild beasts of the earth, that
all the earth may know that there is a God in Israel,
and that all this assembly may know that the LORD
does not deliver by sword or by spear; for the battle
is the LORD'S and He will give you into our hands.

1 SAMUEL 17:45-47

Jehovah Tsaba means the LORD of hosts, or the LORD Our Warrior. Contrary to popular opinion, it was this name that David wielded as a weapon against his enemy, not a rock or a slingshot. That's because David understood that God's name is more than a name; it's a gateway to His power.

David gave the battle to God, "the LORD of hosts" (v. 45). Rather than trying to handle things himself, David recognized God's supremacy in the situation and relied on the LORD to face his giant.

What spiritual resources do you possess because of your relationship with God?

Take time today to thank God for the ways He covers you and equips you for spiritual battles.

DAY 4 How to Approach a Giant

When my oldest granddaughter, Kariss, was a little girl, she was at our house a lot. She called me Poppy, and even though she's in college now, she's still Poppy's girl.

One day when Kariss was younger, she went outside to play. Suddenly I heard her screaming at the top of her lungs, frantic with fear. I immediately rushed outside to see what was wrong. One of our neighbor's dogs was barking at Kariss, and she was paralyzed with terror.

Without a moment's hesitation I scooped up Karris into my arms and held her. Soon her screaming turned to sobs as she calmed down. But then she did something I'll never forget. She looked at me, and then she looked at the dog way down below her. She looked at me again, and then she looked at the dog again. Then she smiled. Her fear was gone.

What happened? The dog hadn't changed. Its bark hadn't changed. Its size hadn't changed. Instead, Kariss's perspective had changed. Because she was now situated high above the dog, she was no longer afraid.

We're studying the story of David and Goliath in order to examine Jehovah Tsaba, the LORD Our Warrior. Today we'll explore two important steps to take when approaching the giants in your life, beginning with a change in your perspective.

Access Your Heavenly Perspective

There are no physical giants walking around in our culture today, although I've met a few professional athletes who come close. Even so, there are many spiritual and emotional giants in our society. Even among Christians, giants rule many of our hearts and homes today because we've lost the ability to look beyond what we see in order to view the spiritual reality surrounding it.

In other words, many of us are experiencing failure and defeat as followers of Christ because we're living with the wrong perspective.

When have you felt frustrated or ineffective as a follower of Christ?

In his letter to the church in Ephesus, Paul wrote that our ultimate perspective on reality shouldn't be based on earth. We shouldn't let our perspective be colored by a society that's hostile to Christianity. Instead, our perspective should come from an entirely different location:

> *God, being rich in mercy, because of His great love with which He loved us, even when we were dead in our transgressions, made us alive together with Christ (by*

grace you have been saved), and raised us up with Him, and seated us with Him in the heavenly places in Christ Jesus.
EPHESIANS 2:4-6

What do these verses teach about our perspective as followers of Christ?

The term "heavenly places" (v. 6) refers to the spiritual realm. As Christians, we're located in two places at once. We exist physically here on earth, and we're also seated with Christ in heaven. Through His death and resurrection Jesus has given us a seat in another location. The problem is that too many Christians focus too much on their earthly location—their earthly perspective—and forget about the fact that they've been raised to heavenly places with Christ.

In our story David's heavenly perspective allowed him to look at Goliath and see not an invincible giant but an *uncircumcised* giant who was ready for a fall (see 1 Sam. 17:26).

How has your salvation influenced your view of your culture and the world around you?

How has your relationship with Christ affected the way you approach problems in life?

As a redeemed son or daughter of Christ, you need to know where you're seated in order to access the power of God's names. You're seated with Christ in the heavenly realm. That reality ought to change the way you view the Goliaths in your life. After all, giants aren't so big when you're looking all the way down from heaven.

So how do we change our perspective? It's not as hard as it sounds. We get caught up in our earthly perspective whenever we focus primarily on earthly concerns—finances, food, relationships, entertainment, physical health, and so on. These aren't necessarily bad things; they're not inherently sinful. But they often distract us from the activities and priorities in our lives that carry spiritual significance.

Regaining our heavenly perspective involves refocusing our energy and our attention on spiritual matters. It means spending time in God's Word, connecting with God through prayer, proclaiming the good news of the gospel, helping the poor, and other disciplines. These kinds of activities lift us up into our Father's arms and allow us to look down at the barking giants on earth with a new perspective and a new confidence for victory.

What habits and activities help you move toward a more heavenly perspective on life?

Advance in God's Name

When you're ready to face a giant in your life, your first step should be to pull your focus away from the earthly realities surrounding that giant and to access a heavenly perspective. Your second step should be to advance and attack in the name of your God, Jehovah Tsaba.

That's what David did during his confrontation with Goliath:

> [David] took his stick in his hand and chose for himself five smooth stones from the brook, and put them in the shepherd's bag which he had, even in his pouch, and his sling was in his hand; **and he approached the Philistine.**
> 1 SAMUEL 17:40, EMPHASIS ADDED

I love the fact that David *approached* the giant. Do you remember what the Israelites did each day when Goliath came out to taunt them? They went in the other direction. They played defense and found a good place to hide. But a powerful Christian doesn't score by playing defense. A powerful Christian advances to face the situation head on.

Do you typically play offense or defense when difficult situations arise in your life? Explain.

Remember that David didn't advance toward Goliath because he was confident in his skills as a warrior or even because he believed himself to be a spiritual giant. David approached Goliath because he was confident in the power of God's names:

> *David said to the Philistine, "You come to me with a sword, a spear, and a javelin, but I come to you in the name of the LORD of hosts [Jehovah Tsaba], the God of the armies of Israel, whom you have taunted."*
>
> **1 SAMUEL 17:45**

Maybe you don't feel confident in your own ability to take down the giants in your life. That's OK. In fact, that's preferable because it means you'll have to rely on God to take them down for you. What you need to do is act in faith.

Choose to move forward. Choose to advance in the name of Jehovah Tsaba, the LORD Our Warrior, and watch Him secure victory where you need it most.

What obstacles have prevented you from taking a leap of faith in the past?

Conclude today's lesson with a time of prayer. Ask God to reveal any situations in which He's ready for you to advance in faith and slay a giant in the power of His name.

DAY 5 How to Kill a Giant

Throughout my decades of pastoral ministry, I've had the honor of serving as the team chaplain for both the Dallas Cowboys and the Dallas Mavericks. I've always approached these roles, first and foremost, as opportunities to advance God's kingdom, but they carry certain perks and privileges as well.

For example, serving as the team chaplain grants me the kind of access that few fans get to experience. If I attempted to walk into the locker room of a professional sports team simply as Tony Evans, I'd probably be banished from the building. But when I approach the locker room as Tony Evans, Team Chaplain, the added title connects my name with a specific role and authority. And that authority grants me the access I need to carry out my role.

In other words, having something extra connected with my name gives me the chance to receive something special.

In a similar way, God has given you the chance to connect something extra to your name. He's issued you the authority to use the power of His names in line with His will. Take advantage of that opportunity!

What privileges have you experienced because of your connection with God?

How do you typically access those privileges?

As we'll see today, David used that authority not only to approach Goliath in God's name but also to slay the giant in God's power. The wonderful news is that you and I have the same opportunity in our lives.

Win by Giving Up

Like the Israelites, many people in the church today are wrestling with the wrong questions. We're so busy trying to figure out how we're supposed to conquer the giants in our lives that we fail to ask ourselves the most important question: *What does God say about this?*

Whenever you spend a lot of time and effort trying to move beyond a difficult situation or overcome opposition—including internal opposition like addiction, fear, or low self-esteem—you know you're operating as if the battle depends on you. Therefore, you're unlikely to succeed.

71

Why? Because the most important battles in your life are spiritual battles. As Paul wrote:

> *Our struggle is not against flesh and blood, but against the rulers, against the powers, against the world forces of this darkness, against the spiritual forces of wickedness in the heavenly places.*

EPHESIANS 6:12

What's your initial reaction to this verse?

Many of the struggles and challenges you face simply stem from living in a fallen world. These can include financial struggles, relational conflict, physical illness, and emotional pain. These kinds of troubles are commonplace, and we have a reasonable chance of overcoming them on our own.

What struggles have you recently faced that you would label as normal?

How confident do you feel about solving these normal troubles?

1	2	3	4	5	6	7	8	9	10
Not confident								**Very confident**	

Yes, there are some difficulties you can handle. But the biggest challenges you'll face in life are strategies Satan sets in motion to trip you up, defeat you, and keep you from reaching the place where God wants you to go. Those challenges are different.

You need to understand that you can't win these kinds of battles—not in your own strength. Satan has your game film. He's studied you. He knows your weaknesses. He knows just how to get you to go where you never thought you'd go and to do what you never thought you'd do. Face it: you're not smart enough or strong enough to defeat an enemy from another realm.

Those battles belong to Jehovah Tsaba.

When have you experienced a difficulty that was beyond your ability to handle?

How did you attempt to overcome that difficulty?

David was able to kill Goliath because he knew the battle wasn't his own (see 1 Sam. 17:47). Once David saw the spiritual core of the physical crisis, he could rest on God's willingness to fight and His ability to win. David knew the hosts of heaven would fight beside him and for him because God is Jehovah Tsaba, the LORD of Hosts.

Yes, David played a part in the victory. But the text takes pains to show us that David's efforts weren't the most important factor:

David put his hand into his bag and took from it a stone and slung it, and struck the Philistine on his forehead. And the stone sank into his forehead, so that he fell on his face to the ground. Thus David prevailed over the Philistine with a sling and a stone, and he struck the Philistine and killed him; but there was no sword in David's hand.
1 SAMUEL 17:49-50

David defeated one of the most fearsome warriors in history, and the passage specifically points out that David didn't even have a sword. This was a divinely orchestrated victory.

Some of the most incredible things God will ever do in your life will occur when you think you have nothing. You think you're not positioned to move forward, make that change, advance in your destiny, defeat that giant—but that's precisely when God is most likely to show up. When He wins your battle, you know who did it. You know who gets the glory. And when the next giant shows up, you know who's going to defeat him—Jehovah Tsaba.

Prepare for the Next Battle

After David killed Goliath, he put him on display:

*David took the Philistine's head and brought it
to Jerusalem, but he put his weapons in his tent.*
1 SAMUEL 17:54

David made a trophy case. When you go to a lodge in the mountains, you might see a room where hunters have displayed the heads of the animals they've killed. In the same way, David wanted to make sure everyone saw what had happened to Goliath.

Why? Because Goliath wasn't the only giant in the land. One giant had been taken down, but that didn't mean another one wasn't lurking around the corner.

How has the church celebrated important spiritual victories over the centuries?

What steps have you taken to celebrate the spiritual victories in your life?

The passage also tells us that David "put his weapons in his tent." It means David put Goliath's weapons in his own tent to let the people know Jehovah Tsaba is able to gain the victory; therefore, they shouldn't fear when the next giant appears. It would serve as a reminder of what God can do in a situation that looks unconquerable to everyone else.

What steps have you taken to remember the great things God has done in your life?

How have God's past victories in your life prepared you to take on the giants you're facing now?

God's name covers it all—past, present, and future. But it especially covers the giants that taunt you. You can trust Jehovah Tsaba to fight for you. The LORD Our Warrior has you covered.

74

CHAPTER 4

JEHOVAH ROHI & JEHOVAH JIREH

INTRODUCTION I Got This

For decades America has been a dominant force in the world on many different levels, including finances, technology, and entertainment. American influence has caused many countries to imitate some of our core ideologies. Sometimes this influence has been positive, such as the emphasis on freedom throughout the world. Sometimes it's been bad, such as the growing plague of consumerism on an international scale.

But one cultural landmark that still keeps America distinct is our emphasis on rugged individualism. As Americans, we love the idea of getting by on our own strength—of pulling ourselves up by our bootstraps and doing whatever needs to be done to succeed. We admire men and women who are strong enough to say, "I don't need any help, thank you. I got this."

We can see this mentality in sports. We love the idea of sports figures who can carry the team on their backs and still achieve victory. Or we often allow individual athletes to overshadow their teams because we place a higher value on individual statistics rather than team success.

The same principle is true in business. We love stories about companies that started in a garage somewhere, struggled for years, and finally broke through to achieve worldwide acclaim. The same is true for movies and TV shows that depict brave men and women fighting through enemy lines or singlehandedly taking on corrupt corporations to build a better world.

In America the individual is king.

Unfortunately, this cultural preference can make it difficult for American Christians to experience the aspects of God we'll focus on this week: the LORD as our Protector and Provider.

DAY 1 Introducing Jehovah Rohi

When I was a child growing up in urban Baltimore, one of my favorite television programs was *Superman*. I loved Superman because he could turn any and every dire situation into a heroic rescue.

As I grew older, Hollywood began turning Superman's story into movies. I went to every one of them, even as an adult. I remember one movie in which my hero delivered a man from a fire. Superman swooped into the burning inferno and rescued the man from certain death. Later, as he was flying across the sky to take the man home, the man was trembling. Superman asked what was wrong, and the man said, "I'm afraid. I'm way up here, and if I fall, I'm going to die."

Superman's response was classic. He said, "Do you think I have enough power to deliver you from the fire but not enough power to deliver you safely home?"

This illustration graphically reflects a similar but more profound truth. Some of us have trusted God to deliver us from the fires of hell, yet we're not sure He can take us safely home. We believe in Him for eternity; we just don't have much confidence in Him for the here and now. We know He will take us to heaven; we're just not sure He's got our back on earth.

What's your initial reaction to the previous statements?

How does your salvation through Jesus equip you for the challenges of daily life?

If you've ever questioned whether God is really on your side, this next name of God is especially for you. The name is found in a psalm that has the power to change your life, a psalm that begins with the phrase "The LORD is my Shepherd" (Ps. 23:1). That name is Jehovah Rohi, which means the LORD My Shepherd.

76

Psalm 23

Let me say up front that I know you're already familiar with Psalm 23. I'm sure you've heard that psalm over and over through the years. I'm sure you've seen it printed on posters and framed in pictures.

But please do me a favor. Don't let your familiarity with Psalm 23 keep you from experiencing its fullest meaning for your life. In fact, take a moment right now to mentally step back, take a deep breath, and encounter this important psalm once again with an open mind:

> *The LORD is my shepherd,*
> *I shall not want.*
> *He makes me lie down in green pastures;*
> *He leads me beside quiet waters.*
> *He restores my soul;*
> *He guides me in the paths of righteousness*
> *For His name's sake.*
> *Even though I walk through*
> *the valley of the shadow*
> *   of death,*
> *I fear no evil, for You are with me;*
> *Your rod and Your staff, they comfort me.*
> *You prepare a table before*
> *me in the presence*
> *   of my enemies;*
> *You have anointed my head with oil;*
> *My cup overflows.*
> *Surely goodness and lovingkindness*
> *   will follow me all the days of my life,*
> *And I will dwell in the house*
> *of the LORD forever.*

PSALM 23:1-6

What emotions do you experience when you read these verses?

What do you appreciate most in this psalm? Why?

The name of God translated LORD in this psalm is Jehovah, the Self-Revealing One. The Hebrew term for *shepherd* is the word *rohi* or *ra'ah*, which means *to tend, pasture, shepherd*.

If you're wondering why David, the author of this psalm, painted a picture of God as a Shepherd of sheep, remember David had a lot of experience with sheep. Before he was King David, he was David the shepherd. He looked back over the span of his life, remembered what it was like to tend sheep, and recognized ways God had tended him like a Shepherd over the years. So David used his experiences in his old job to describe his relationship with God. As a result, he produced one of the most beautiful, practical poems in all Scripture.

How have your major life experiences helped you understand God more fully?

Over the next few days we'll highlight six principles from Psalm 23 that can help us live in the power of the name Jehovah Rohi. But today let's explore two important words that set the tone for this psalm.

God Our Shepherd

I don't have a lot of experience with sheep, and there's a pretty good chance you don't either. If you live in an urban environment, as I do, you may never have seen a real sheep in your life. But you can still understand the role and function of a shepherd. To put it simply, a shepherd's job is to take care of sheep.

That's a simple statement, but it has huge implications for our relationship with God. Because if God is our Shepherd—if He's Jehovah Rohi—then we are His sheep. And we can be confident that He will take care of us.

How confident do you feel about God's role in taking care of you?

1   2   3   4   5   6   7   8   9   10

Not confident   **Very confident**

People today look to all kinds of things to take care of them. Some look to their money. Others look to their power. Others look to relationships, success, the government, and so on. Worst of all, many people believe they're fully capable of taking care of themselves. They feel they've got everything under control.

Not David. He said, "The LORD is my Shepherd" (v. 1). David used two words that deserve our attention.

1. Notice the way David used the present tense when describing his situation. He didn't say, "The LORD *used to be* my Shepherd." He didn't say, "The LORD *will be* my Shepherd when I get to heaven." No, he said, "The LORD *is* my Shepherd" (v. 1, emphasis added). He acknowledged the fact that God was taking care of him even as he wrote those words. God takes care of us in every moment of every day.

   What or whom do you typically trust to take care of you instead of God?

   What steps can you take to remember and focus on God's care throughout each day?

2. The second word I want you to notice is *my*. David wrote, "The LORD is *my* Shepherd" (v. 1, emphasis added). In other words, David identified God as his personal Shepherd. It's true that God is interested in the entire flock of Christians known as the church, but He also cares about each individual sheep in the flock. He stands ready not simply as *the* Shepherd but as *my* Shepherd and as *your* Shepherd.

79

Do you see why I encouraged you not to overlook this psalm? We haven't even finished the first verse, and we've already seen potent evidence that Jehovah Rohi is a personal Shepherd and a right-now God. There's much more to come.

DAY 2 The Shepherd's Care

We're studying Jehovah Rohi, the LORD My Shepherd. And if you want to come away with a good understanding of God as your Shepherd, you need to start by understanding yourself as one of His sheep. That's important. Because if you can't condescend to think of yourself as a sheep, you'll never be able to fully experience all your Shepherd has in store for you.

The first thing you need to know about sheep is this: sheep are dumb. It wouldn't be too much of an exaggeration to say that sheep are the dumbest animals in all creation. In fact, sheep are so dumb that if one sheep starts walking around in a circle, another sheep will follow it, and then another, and then another until the whole flock is walking around in a circle, with all the sheep thinking they're headed somewhere.

Sheep are also defenseless. If a sheep meets a wolf or a coyote in the wilderness, it's over. The sheep is already dead because it has no effective method for fighting off an attacker. Its only hope is the shepherd.

In addition, sheep are dirty. They have no way to clean their wool when it gets matted with dirt, sweat, or worse.

Finally, sheep are dependent. Because they're directionally challenged, they must be led by the shepherd if they want to go anywhere.

Keep those truths in mind when you consider these words by the prophet Isaiah:

All of us like sheep have gone astray,
Each of us has turned to his own way;
But the LORD has caused
the iniquity of us all
To fall on Him.
ISAIAH 53:6

What's your initial reaction to this verse?

What are some ways we act like sheep as followers of Christ?

You and I are sheep who need a Shepherd. So let's go back to Psalm 23 and identify some of the benefits we receive from Jehovah Rohi.

"I Shall Not Want"

After identifying God as his Shepherd—Jehovah Rohi—David added the phrase "I shall not want" (v. 1). In other words, David's Shepherd, the LORD, has covered all his needs. This is true for a good shepherd who tends to the needs of his sheep, and it's also true of our LORD, who tends to each of our needs. He has us comprehensively covered.

How has God met your needs in recent years?

God identifies Himself as the Shepherd of His people at other places in Scripture. Look here, for example:

"I Myself will gather the remnant of My flock out of all the countries where I have driven them and bring them back to their pasture, and they will be fruitful and multiply. I will also raise up shepherds over them and they will tend them; and they will not be afraid any longer, nor be terrified, nor will any be missing," declares the LORD.
JEREMIAH 23:3-4

Similarly, Ezekiel 34 explains what God expects a shepherd to do among His people.

Read Ezekiel 34:1-4. Record the responsibilities listed in these verses for those who serve as shepherds of God's people.

How do shepherds in the church meet these responsibilities today?

Most importantly, Jesus offered His own take on what it means to be a shepherd dedicated to meeting the needs of the sheep:

> *I am the good shepherd; the good shepherd
> lays down His life for the sheep.*
>
> **JOHN 10:11**

In what ways has Jesus met your needs as your Good Shepherd?

When you're selecting a shepherd for your life, you can identify a good one by his willingness to sacrifice his life for you. You know Jesus is such a Shepherd because He already gave up His life to deliver you from sin and to give you eternal life.

As our Shepherd, Jehovah Rohi has met our needs for wisdom, defense, spiritual cleanliness, and direction, just to name a few. Most importantly, He's met our need for salvation. We "shall not want" (Ps. 23:1) for all eternity.

"He Restores My Soul"

Most of us know what it's like to have a flat tire. But did you know you can also have a flat soul? This means your spiritual get-up-and-go has got up and gone.

Some people have simply lost the fire in their soul. They drag themselves to church—if they go at all—from a sense of guilt or routine. Others have punctured their own soul because of poor choices; they've deflated their soul through sin. Others have lost their connection with God through a variety of circumstances, as if He's far away on vacation and they don't know where to find Him.

How would you describe the condition of your soul in recent months?

1   2   3   4   5   6   7   8   9   10

My soul is flat.   **My soul is healthy.**

The good news is that flat souls can be restored. That's what David experienced, according to these verses:

> *He makes me lie down in green pastures;*
> *He leads me beside quiet waters.*
> *He restores my soul.*
> **PSALM 23:2-3**

Notice Jehovah Rohi used two methods to restore David's soul.

1. David wrote, "He makes me lie down in green pastures" (v. 2). Don't miss the emphasis on that word *makes*. This wasn't a suggestion or a voluntary action on David's part. God forced David to be still and totally rely on Him.

Have you considered maybe God hasn't changed your difficult situation because He's waiting for you to relinquish your rebellion, let go of your self-sufficiency, and lie down? He's willing to keep you where you are until you've learned to rest in Him—until you declare your total trust in Him and total dependence on Him.

How would you benefit from a season of rest and reliance on God?

What obstacles have prevented you from taking that step?

2. David also wrote that God "leads me beside quiet waters" (v. 2). I found this to be very interesting about sheep: they won't drink from running water. They are afraid (and rightfully so) of stumbling into a brook or stream and drowning. They drink only from still pools. Therefore, shepherds often carve out a small channel from a running-water source to create "quiet waters" for their sheep.

When we rest in the LORD our Shepherd, He leads us to environments we can handle. He provides green grass and still water for our spiritual restoration. Unfortunately, you won't discover the blessing of rest and still waters as long as you remain self-sufficient. You won't experience Jehovah Rohi as long as you think you can fix your problems yourself—as long as you wander off on your own path.

How can you identify and eliminate patterns of self-sufficiency in your life?

Spend time in prayer with Jehovah Rohi. Thank Him for being the Good Shepherd who provides for you, restores your soul, and leads you beside quiet waters. Ask Him to show you any patterns of self-sufficiency in your life. Confess your dependence on Him and entrust your soul to His care.

As David discovered—and as we can discover—God will restore our soul when we recognize our place as a member of His flock.

DAY 3 The Shepherd's Guidance

Unlike many of my friends and family members, I have yet to be fully convinced of the advantages of modern technology. I mentioned earlier that I don't use a computer, and to be honest, I don't feel I'm missing much. I do OK by keeping things old-school.

What are the main ways technology has affected your life?

Would you characterize that impact as positive or negative? Explain your response.

In spite of my aversion to technology, I've found one device useful on more than one occasion: the navigation system in my car. It uses a global-positioning system (GPS) to connect with a satellite in outer space. And because that satellite can view the entire landscape of the earth around me, it knows how to guide me from where I am to wherever I want to go.

This ability to guide us from on high points to a central quality of Jehovah Rohi, the LORD Our Shepherd.

"Paths of Righteousness"

If we rely on machines that see everything in order to guide us on a physical level, then surely we can understand the need for God to guide us on spiritual and emotional levels. After all, God is the Creator of all things and is intimately aware of everything that's happening in our lives. He knows where we should be going—even when we don't—and He has the ability to lead us there.

David understood this reality:

> *He guides me in the paths of righteousness*
> *For His name's sake.*
> **PSALM 23:3**

When has God directed you in a meaningful way?

What are "the paths of righteousness" in your life?

A shepherd needs to guide his sheep because they're prone to wander. They're dumb, remember? They take wrong turns when left to their own devices.

In the same way, you and I can look back on our lives and identify some wrong turns and unwise decisions. In hindsight we can see the paths of righteousness with greater clarity, and we can also identify the many times we wandered away from those paths and chose to go our own way.

The wonderful thing about Jehovah Rohi is that He's able to guide us toward the proper paths on the front end. When we trust God as our Shepherd, we don't have to wait for hindsight. He's willing to lead us on the right path in every decision we face, and He's willing to return us to the right path if we've wandered off—but only if we choose to seek and follow Him.

What obstacles have prevented you from following God's direction?

Let's keep in mind that this world isn't filled with only good paths and neutral paths. One reason we desperately need Jehovah Rohi on our side is that He can also lead us when we find ourselves on evil paths in the valleys of life.

"I Fear No Evil"

We've reached one of the most famous verses in all Scripture:

> *Even though I walk through the valley*
> *of the shadow of death,*
> *I fear no evil, for You are with me;*
> *Your rod and Your staff, they comfort me.*
> **PSALM 23:4**

What emotions do you experience when you read that verse? Why?

Valleys are low places between mountains. They're often filled with vulnerability and risk, especially for sheep. One reason sheep often feel afraid in valleys is that one of the mountains on either side frequently blocks the sun. Sheep often associate these shadows with the coming of night, when foxes, wolves, and other predators come out.

Yet David assures us in this psalm that even in the valley that casts the shadow of death, Jehovah Rohi is ready to provide comfort and protection. He guides us through the valley with His presence, His rod, and His staff.

When have you recently been through a valley?

How have you experienced God's presence and protection in the darker seasons of your life?

Everyone wants to live on the mountaintop. We want times when our job is good, our health is good, our family is good, and our faith is good. Unfortunately, we can't jump from mountaintop to mountaintop as we journey through life. We all go through the valley.

Don't miss that word *through*. David wrote, "Even though I walk *through* the valley" (v. 4, emphasis added). He didn't write, "Even though I sit down and whine in the valley." He didn't write, "Even though I give up and go back because of the valley." In order to reach the next mountain, you need to go *through* the valley you find yourself in. When the going gets tough, you need to keep going, because the only way *out* is *through*.

Thankfully, we don't walk on our own. Jehovah Rohi is with us. Our Shepherd will guide us through.

"My Cup Overflows"

One truth that motivates us to walk through the valleys is the knowledge that God, our Shepherd, has good things prepared for us ahead:

> *You prepare a table before me in the*
> *   presence of my enemies;*
> *You have anointed my head with oil;*
> *My cup overflows.*
> **PSALM 23:5**

In David's time, beginning in early spring, shepherds scoped out the mountain ranges for new grazing land. They located broad, elevated land with plenty of grass and then began preparing the area for the arrival of their sheep. Shepherds spread minerals over the land and removed any poisonous plants. They surveyed the area for snakes and guarded against natural enemies of the sheep, such as foxes, wolves, and hyenas. In these ways shepherds prepared the tableland for the arrival of the sheep and for their sustenance throughout the summer grazing season.

That's what verse 5 is referring to when it says the LORD Himself prepares a table for us. In His presence we're safe from our enemies. That's because God isn't subject to our enemies; He's bigger than all of them put together. He knows how to provide for us even in the midst of a bad situation.

How do you currently spend time in God's presence?

What steps can you take to seek God's presence more fully when you experience attacks from your enemies?

When we bask in the presence of Jehovah Rohi, our "cup overflows" (v. 5). We have more than we need because of His abounding goodness to us.

How has your cup overflowed in recent years?

David ended his poem by declaring that God, Jehovah Rohi, meets our spiritual needs as well as our physical and emotional needs:

> Surely goodness and
> lovingkindness will follow
>   me all the days of my life,
> And I will dwell in the house
> of the LORD forever.
>
> **PSALM 23:6**

When the LORD is your Shepherd, He's got you covered. He's got your back. He will care for your needs in this life, and He will guide you through the valleys to a place far greater than you've ever imagined. That's the power and provision of Jehovah Rohi.

Praise God today as Jehovah Rohi. Ask Him to guide you on paths of righteousness. Thank Him for guiding you through any valley you're walking through.

DAY 4 Introducing Jehovah Jireh

All of us have had moments in our lives that defined us or served as key turning points in our direction and purpose. Strangely enough, many of those moments are connected with the painful trials and tests God sometimes allows to come our way.

For example, when I was a young man growing up in urban Baltimore, I had no idea that one of the defining moments in my life would take place during an unexpected trial. It happened on a football field called The Diamond, which was only a few blocks from my home.

God works in unusual ways. On that day as I ran toward the end zone with the football, a simple cross-body block snapped my right leg in two. (I still have the steel plate in my leg from the surgery.) I remember lying on the ground in excruciating pain, waiting for the ambulance to arrive. In that moment I knew God was sovereign and His will and His way are perfect, even when He asks us to give up something we love.

I said, "God, You know I love football more than anything. But I'm going to thank You in the middle of this pain and loss. I know You have a plan for my life, and I give You my life to fulfill Your plan." Not long after that, God sealed in me a commitment to full-time ministry, and there's been no turning back.

What are some of the key turning points in your life?

How have those turning points influenced your relationship with God?

As we'll see in today's lesson, Abraham's life was also turned upside down during an intense test of his faith. Through that test he experienced God in a new way and came to know Him as Jehovah Jireh, the LORD Our Provider.

Abraham's Test

The Book of Genesis provides the backdrop for Abraham's difficult test and for the revelation of our next compound connection:

> *God tested Abraham, and said to him, "Abraham!" And he said, "Here I am." He said, "Take now your son, your only son, whom you love, Isaac, and go to the land of Moriah, and offer him there as a burnt offering on one of the mountains of which I will tell you."*
> **GENESIS 22:1-2**

What's your initial reaction to these verses?

When have you had to give up something in order to obey God?

The passage specifically tells us God tested Abraham in the most devastating way possible. He asked Abraham to give Him the one thing Abraham loved most—his son. Isaac was Abraham's dream come true. He was the promised and long-awaited gift from God, and now God was asking for him back.

Read the following passages of Scripture and record what they teach about Abraham and Isaac.

Genesis 12:1-4

Genesis 15:1-6

Genesis 21:1-8

On the surface these passages suggest God's command to Abraham in Genesis 22 didn't make sense. In fact, it appeared God was contradicting His own promise.

As a result, Abraham found himself deep in a mess of contradictions. He was in a theological contradiction because God's command to sacrifice Isaac went against God's promise of a future nation. He was in an emotional contradiction because his faith was colliding with his affections. He was in a social contradiction because he deeply desired to become the "great nation" (12:2) God had promised. And he was in a relational contradiction because sacrificing Isaac would undoubtedly create a great strain on his marriage.

Abraham was up a creek without a paddle. He was in a big-time trial.

The Nature of Trials

We'll conclude Abraham's story in tomorrow's material, but I want to camp here for a moment to consider the nature of the trials we experience as followers of Christ. And that's the first thing we need to understand: we *all* experience trials as followers of Christ. You're not the only one.

Trials are adverse circumstances God introduces or allows in order to identify our spiritual state and to prepare us for the direction in which He wants to take us. If you're alive, you can't escape trials in this life. Either you're in a trial now, you've just come out of a trial, or you're getting ready to go into a trial.

Even Jesus spoke about the unavoidable nature of trials in this life:

> *I have told you these things, so that in me you may have peace. In this world you will have trouble. But take heart! I have overcome the world.*
> **JOHN 16:33, NIV**

What trials are you walking through right now?

How have those trials affected you on an emotional level?

How have those trials affected you on a spiritual level?

Jesus' words point to the second truth we need to understand about trials: they fall under God's jurisdiction. Nobody likes enduring trials, but we can take comfort in the knowledge that trials must first pass through God's hands before reaching us—that nothing comes our way without first receiving God's divine seal of approval. And if God has approved a circumstance in our lives, He can use that circumstance to create something good.

That's why many biblical writers encourage us to view trials as a reason for joy rather than sorrow. Here's an example from the Book of James:

Consider it all joy, my brethren, when you encounter various trials, knowing that the testing of your faith produces endurance. And let endurance have its perfect result, so that you may be perfect and complete, lacking in nothing.

JAMES 1:2-4

What's your response to the idea of finding joy during trials?

When we look back at Abraham's situation, we can see that his particular trial was also a test. God wanted to know exactly where Abraham's heart and faith stood, so He gave Abraham a command designed to find out.

I know how Abraham must have felt. Back at The Diamond, everyone watching that football game saw a kid with a broken leg. Yet for me, the trial unveiled a new name of God—Jehovah Jireh—and a new direction for my life. Unfortunately, many of us miss the purpose behind our tests because we become fixated on the circumstances and stress involved.

What steps can you take to retain your focus on God during trials?

Abraham was in the midst of a terrible test. He faced a choice between the blessing and the Blesser, and God wanted to see which he would choose. God wanted to know whether Abraham would let go of his most valued possession and simply worship Him, even when it hurt. As we'll see tomorrow, that's exactly what Abraham did.

DAY 5 Trusting Our Provider

If you have children or grandchildren, I can almost guarantee you've heard them ask, "How many days until Christmas?" For millions of people, Christmas Day is the pinnacle of a glorious season of celebration and gift giving. It's celebrated in many cultures around the world, with each one adding its own ethnic traditions, food, and music.

Of course, at the heart of Christmas is the reminder that Jesus came to earth as God's ultimate Gift—our Redeemer and Savior. Jesus' coming blessed us with the opportunity to have a relationship with a perfect, loving Father who calls us His children.

What do you like best about the Christmas season? Why?

But we must remember something about God. It's a characteristic He shares with every parent. He doesn't want us to love Him only for His gifts. Imagine your kids wanting to be with you only because they knew they'd receive a big payoff on Christmas Day. You wouldn't like that. As a parent, you give to your children because you love them, not to bribe them into loving you back.

The same is true of God. He loves us; therefore, He gives us good gifts. But He wants us to love Him apart from His gifts. God isn't a genie or a cosmic bellhop. He loves giving from His hand as long as He knows we're really after His heart.

What steps can we take to avoid defining God based only on His gifts to us?

Yesterday we saw that God tested Abraham to confirm the motives of his heart. Today we'll see that Abraham's response helped him experience God as Jehovah Jireh and understand once and for all that the LORD provides.

A Strong Faith

In Genesis 22 God commanded Abraham to sacrifice his only son, Isaac, as a burnt offering in the land of Moriah. It's important to note that Abraham was quick to obey:

> *Abraham rose early in the morning and saddled his donkey, and took two of his young men with him and Isaac his son; and he split wood for the burnt offering, and arose and went to the place of which God had told him. On the third day Abraham raised his eyes and saw the place from a distance.*
>
> **GENESIS 22:3-4**

What do these verses teach us about Abraham?

Notice the text doesn't say Abraham attempted to bargain with God or even ask why. The text doesn't record Abraham's extended laments that life was unfair, nor does it say Abraham sneaked a spare lamb into his baggage just in case. Instead, Abraham "rose," "saddled," "took," "split," and "went."

When Isaac questioned Abraham about the lamb for the sacrifice, Abraham expressed his confidence that God would provide:

> *Isaac spoke to Abraham his father and said, "My father!" And he said, "Here I am, my son." And he said, "Behold, the fire and the wood, but where is the lamb for the burnt offering?" Abraham said, "God will provide for Himself the lamb for the burnt offering, my son."*
>
> **GENESIS 22:7-8**

Where did Abraham find the strength and the faith to respond so decisively to what seemed like an unfair command from God? We find the answer in the New Testament Book of Hebrews:

> *By faith Abraham, when he was tested, offered up Isaac, and he who had received the promises was offering up his only begotten son; it was he to whom it was said, "In Isaac your descendants shall be called." He considered that God is able to raise people even from the dead, from which he also received him back as a type.*
> **HEBREWS 11:17-19**

What do these verses teach us about Abraham?

Abraham knew his situation was hopeless by human standards, and yet he chose to hope in his God. Abraham believed God is good, and he chose to trust that God would provide something good in a bad situation, even to the point of producing a miracle and raising Isaac from the dead.

When have you been able to trust God with something you didn't fully understand? What happened next?

What factors prevent you from trusting God more fully?

Abraham trusted God, and Jehovah Jireh responded by resolving the situation in an unexpected way.

An Unexpected Provision

Look at what happened at the climax of this story:

Abraham stretched out his hand and took the knife to slay his son. But the angel of the LORD called to him from heaven and said, "Abraham, Abraham!" And he said, "Here I am." He said, "Do not stretch out your hand against the lad, and do nothing to him; for now I know that you fear God, since you have not withheld your son, your only son, from Me." Then Abraham raised his eyes and looked, and behold, behind him a ram caught in the thicket by his horns; and Abraham went and took the ram and offered him up for a burnt offering in the place of his son.

GENESIS 22:10-13

Abraham experienced the miraculous provision of God. It didn't happen the way he expected it to happen, and it certainly wasn't a positive or comfortable situation in any way—not when he had to stretch out his hand and hold a knife over his son. In the end Abraham's faith opened the door to a new experience with God.

In what ways has your faith been tested in the past?

How has God revealed more about Himself during your tests of faith?

I love the idea that while Abraham was enduring the terrible trial of climbing up that mountain, the ram God intended to substitute for Isaac was climbing up the opposite slope at the same time. God was sovereign over the problem and the solution, and He knew exactly how to match them at exactly the right time.

The same principle can apply to you and me. Often the answer to the trial we're facing is sitting right next to us, but we'll never see it until God's ready to reveal it. That's why we need to remain focused on Him and trust Him for His provision.

Why are we so often tempted to find our own solutions rather than staying focused on God?

Read Romans 5:8. How has Christ provided for you in ways you couldn't have expected?

Watch how Abraham responded to God's provision:

Abraham went and took the ram and offered him up for a burnt offering in the place of his son. Abraham called the name of that place The LORD Will Provide, as it is said to this day, "In the mount of the LORD it will be provided."

GENESIS 22:13-14

We all have our own Isaac. It's that thing we desire more than life itself. Your Isaac is whatever you least want to release—whatever makes you hold on most tightly at even the slightest suggestion of letting go.

Are you willing to let go? Are you willing to trust God completely, even with your Isaac? If so, you'll experience Jehovah Jireh—the LORD Will Provide—as Abraham did. If not, you'll continue throwing your own solutions at trials and tests that find their solutions only in God.

God longs to be Jehovah Jireh to you today. But He wants to know and see that you're willing to obey Him, to seek Him, and not to place anything above Him as more important in your life. When He sees you honor Him that way, as Abraham did, you'll also discover the power of Jehovah Jireh in your life.

Is there anything in your life that's keeping you from completely trusting in God's provision? If so, spend time with Jehovah Jireh and ask Him to increase your faith and teach you to trust Him as your Provider, even in your trials. Thank Him for providing your salvation through the sacrifice of His Son.

CHAPTER 5

EL ELYON & EL SHADDAI

INTRODUCTION Big and Bigger

The world today is bigger than it's ever been, and it's growing larger all the time. I'm not talking about physical size, of course, since our planet hasn't grown larger. Nor am I talking about the size of our human population, although that certainly continues to skyrocket with each passing year.

When I say the world is bigger than it's ever been, I'm talking about the relative bigness connected with various elements of modern life. For example, buildings are bigger than they've ever been. At over 2,700 feet high, the Burj Khalifa in Dubai is the world's tallest building as I write these words, but there are already rumors about and plans for larger buildings to surpass it in the coming years.

The bigness of the world goes beyond physical structures. Economies and nations are bigger than they've ever been. Many countries around the world—not just the United States—have huge resources at their disposal. They can throw their weight around during international political discussions and demand to be heard.

The same is true of modern businesses with global networks and multinational interests. And we can't neglect mentioning worldwide celebrities with their oversized influence and egos—both of which are amplified through the power of technology and social media.

Do you see what I mean? The world is big, and it's growing bigger every day. But we must always remember that God is bigger still. As we'll see this week, God is higher than anything we could hope to construct—the Most High God. And God is more powerful than any person, nation, or corporation—God Almighty.

Join me in exploring those realities as we focus on two more names of God: El Elyon and El Shaddai.

DAY 1 Introducing El Elyon

In 2010 a group of 33 Chilean miners was trapped 2,300 feet underground in a copper and gold mine just outside Copiapó, Chile. A cave-in had blocked the exit deep in the earth, imprisoning them in a fortress of rock.

For more than two weeks, the miners had no contact with the outside world. They saw nothing except darkness and heard nothing other than their own voices. Now it's bad enough being in a pit, but it's even worse when you can't get out and you can't make contact with anyone. The miners were helpless and desperate. Their only hope was that help would somehow come from above.

Finally, after 17 days the miners taped a note to one of the drills sent down by rescue workers more than two thousand feet above them on the surface. Quickly, the rescue workers drilled a larger hole in the same spot, then inserted a small tube through which they provided the miners with food, water, light, medicine, and communication equipment.

The tube didn't deliver the miners from their dire circumstances, but it offered something they desperately needed: it gave them hope.

How do you define the word *hope*?

Where do you typically search for hope when you need it?

We'll finish the story of the Chilean miners tomorrow, but today we need to pause and deal with the desperate circumstances in which we sometimes find ourselves. Maybe you're going through such an experience. You've probably never set foot in a copper mine or a gold mine, but life may have caved in on you financially, relationally, emotionally, physically, or spiritually.

In other words, like the miners, you may be in a situation in which you see no way out. You're trapped, and you're not sure anyone up above even knows where you are.

When have you been in a situation in which you felt there was no way out?

Knowing God's names won't automatically or immediately remove the negative circumstances from your life. But as Abraham discovered, we feel more confident and hopeful when we understand the true nature of the One who's above all things. That's El Elyon—the Most High God.

A Courageous Rescue

You probably recognize the names of the cities Sodom and Gomorrah because of God's fiery judgment on their inhabitants, recorded in Genesis 19. Years earlier, however, the people of those cities needed help in a very different predicament.

The evil king Chedorlaomer, the ruler of Elam, and three other power-hungry kings faced off against five kings who were merely seeking to defend their livelihoods, countrymen, and homes. Two of the five defending kings represented the cities of Sodom and Gomorrah.

The nine kings waged war in the valley of Siddim, which contained several tar pits at the time. As the battle escalated, the five defensive kings were forced to retreat. The kings of Sodom and Gomorrah, along with their armies, became trapped in the tar pits. Their people were taken captive by Chedorlaomer's forces, and all their possessions were confiscated.

Read Genesis 14:8-16. What stands out to you about Abraham's actions?

Where do you see God in these verses?

You may be thinking, *What does this have to do with any-thing? Why does the Bible even record this story?* The answer is that Abraham's nephew, Lot, was one of the prisoners.

When Abraham (also called Abram) learned of Lot's situation, he wasted no time launching a rescue mission:

> *When Abram heard that his relative had been taken captive, he led out his trained men, born in his house, three hundred and eighteen, and went in pursuit as far as Dan. He divided his forces against them by night, he and his servants, and defeated them, and pursued them as far as Hobah, which is north of Damascus. He brought back all the goods, and also brought back his relative Lot with his possessions, and also the women, and the people.*
> **GENESIS 14:14-16**

When have you recently been called on to rescue or help a friend in need?

When have you recently needed rescue or help?

Abraham made it clear that nobody was to mess with his people. With 318 trained men he chased down the enemy over a 240-mile span—and all without a single vehicle. So there you have it: Abraham courageously responded to an injustice and saved the day. End of story.

Or was it? As we further explore the text, we meet an interesting individual, Melchizedek, who adds another layer to Abraham's experience.

God Most High

After the King of Sodom had been released from captivity, he met Abraham in the Valley of Shaveh, also called the King's Valley (see v. 17). There he introduced Abraham to another king named Melchizedek. The text tells us Melchizedek was the king of Salem.

Look what happened next:

*Melchizedek king of Salem brought
out bread and wine; now he was a
priest of God Most High [El Elyon].
He blessed him and said,
"Blessed be Abram of God
Most High [El Elyon],
Possessor of heaven and earth;
And blessed be God Most High [El Elyon],
Who has delivered your
enemies into your hand."*

GENESIS 14:18-20

What do these verses teach us about God?

What do these verses teach about the battle between Abraham and the other kings?

There's our next name of God—El Elyon. To determine the meaning of this name, we need to understand that El is the abbreviated form of Elohim. And if you remember from week 1, Elohim was the name connected with God during creation, referring to His power. Elohim is the strong Creator God.

When El is combined with the Hebrew term Elyon, the compound connection refers to God as the Highest or the Most. The literal translation is Most Exalted High God.

In other words, El Elyon tells us God is high above everything else, including our enemies or any problems that cause us pain. Therefore, El Elyon can be a Source of hope who sees our desperate situation and sends help from on high. That's what David learned about God:

*I will cry to God Most High [El Elyon],
To God who accomplishes all things for me.
He will send from heaven and save me;
He reproaches him who tramples upon me.
God will send forth His
lovingkindness and His truth.*

PSALM 57:2-3

102

In your experience what does it mean to "cry to God Most High" (v. 2)?

What are the benefits of calling out to God when you're in need?

Why did God reveal Himself as El Elyon during this particular moment in history? The answer has a lot to do with the backdrop of Abraham's battle. Remember, the war involved nine separate kings at the head of their armies. Abraham and Melchizedek met in the King's Valley, along with the King of Sodom. Melchizedek himself was the king of Salem.

Are you catching the theme? Genesis 14 features a whole mess of kings. But over and above them all is El Elyon, the Most High God. He's the One who secured victory for Abraham, and He's the One to whom we can turn whenever we need rescue and hope.

Spend time today praising God as El Elyon—the Most High God. Cry out to Him about any desperate situation you're experiencing and ask Him to help you.

DAY 2 The Glory of El Elyon

Yesterday we began the story of 33 Chilean miners who were trapped 2,300 feet underground after a catastrophic cave-in. The miners had no contact with the outside world for 17 days before they finally attached a note to a drill operated by rescue workers. The miners were alive, but they needed help.

That help arrived first in the form of a tube that delivered food, water, medicine, light, and communication with the rescuers above. This was undoubtedly a blessing for the miners, but it didn't solve their problem. They were still stuck.

Rescue finally arrived in the form of a two-foot-wide capsule called the Phoenix. Lowered through a vertical shaft, the Phoenix lifted the miners one by one from their underground prison. Amazingly, all 33 men were saved.

After the rescue one of the miners said the group had gathered together in the pit and called on God to rescue them. They appealed to His name and the character attached to it. The miners hadn't placed all their hopes on the rescuers located 2,300 feet above them. They weren't focused only on their earthly hope of assistance. They'd also depended on their Rescuer who was located all the way up. They appealed to El Elyon—God Most High.

Like Abraham, the miners believed God could see their situation and hear their cries for help, and they were right. El Elyon heard, and He arranged for their rescue before it was too late.

Do you ever feel God is too far beyond you to hear or care about your prayers? Explain.

Which of your prayers has God answered in recent years? Record at least three.

1.

2.

3.

It's one thing to believe God is high above everything else. But it's another matter to match your actions with that belief. Thankfully, this was another area in which Abraham proved to be a man of great integrity and faith.

Acknowledging God's Glory

At the end of Genesis 14, Abraham demonstrated his intrinsic understanding of God's character, holiness, and might. After an encouraging conversation with Melchizedek, the king of Salem, Abraham had a less beneficial chat with the King of Sodom:

*The king of Sodom said to Abram, "Give the people to me
and take the goods for yourself." Abram said to the king of
Sodom, "I have sworn to the LORD God Most High, possessor
of heaven and earth, that I will not take a thread or a sandal
thong or anything that is yours, for fear you would say, 'I
have made Abram rich.' I will take nothing except what the
young men have eaten, and the share of the men who went
with me, Aner, Eshcol, and Mamre; let them take their share."*

GENESIS 14:21-24

What do we learn about Abraham from these verses?

No doubt the king of Sodom was pleased with what
Abraham had accomplished, but he also saw an opportunity. Knowing Abraham was a force to be reckoned with, he
wanted to strike a deal. He offered to let Abraham and his
men keep the loot from the vanquished armies, while the
king of Sodom would leave with the captured soldiers.

The first problem with the king of Sodom's pitch was that
he forgot he'd lost the battle. He'd been a captive who needed
rescue; therefore, he was in no position to set terms or offer
deals. The second problem was that he wanted to horn in on
the credit for the victory. Why did the king want Abraham to
"give the people to [him] and take the goods" (v. 21)? Because
the king wanted the glory of leading captured soldiers
through the gates of his city. He wanted a victory parade so
that people would think he'd won the war. In other words, the
king of Sodom wanted part of the glory for himself.

That was a problem for Abraham, because he recognized that God deserved credit for the victory—and God
alone. Melchizedek had come to the same conclusion a few
verses earlier:

> *Blessed be Abram of God Most High,*
> *Possessor of heaven and earth;*
> *And blessed be God Most High,*
> *Who has delivered your*
> *enemies into your hand.*

GENESIS 14:19-20

Both Abraham and Melchizedek understood that God is the ultimate Source of the victories in our lives. When we accomplish something important, we do so because we're fueled by power from on high. We're supported by El Elyon. Therefore, it's vital for us to offer the glory for those accomplishments back to God, as Abraham did.

What does it mean practically for us to give God the glory for His victories and accomplishments in our lives?

What are some ways we might try to keep God's glory for ourselves?

Implications of the Name El Elyon

There's power in approaching God as El Elyon—God Most High. But how does this name affect our lives? Why is it important for us today? Let's look at three implications of this name.

1. If you're like me, you regularly encounter people who believe themselves to be high on the food chain. You know people who have a higher rank than you at work. You see people who have more money or more worldly possessions than you. And I'm sure you come across people who have more recognition, power, or influence than you. That's life for almost every follower of Christ.

Yet I want you to remember that no matter how high up a person may be, El Elyon is still higher. El Elyon is the Maker of heaven and earth, and He ultimately calls the shots. He has the final say. No one is higher than El Elyon, and that means He puts everyone in their place, including you and me.

How would you rate your influence and power in your normal spheres of life?

| 1 | 2 | 3 | 4 | 5 | 6 | 7 | 8 | 9 | 10 |

No influence   **Great influence**

What are the implications of acknowledging God as El Elyon for your daily actions and attitudes?

2. God's identity as El Elyon makes it important to root out any idolatry in our lives. Most Christians don't think they struggle with idolatry, because most Christians don't worship carvings made of wood or stone. But the reality is that anytime you lift something or someone higher than God, you create an idol. To worship an idol is to prioritize something above the Most High God.

   What steps can you take to evaluate your heart for any traces of idolatry?

3. To understand God as El Elyon also means we recognize that He has the right to overrule. In Abraham and Lot's case God used 318 men to overrule a collection of mighty kings and overpower their armies. The odds certainly weren't in Abraham's favor. Neither were the circumstances. Yet 318 men plus one El Elyon are more than enough to defeat humanity's biggest armies, because El Elyon is Most High over heaven and earth.

   How often do you allow the size of a problem to prevent you from seeking a solution?

Never look first at the odds against you. The odds won't give you the final story. Never focus on the size of the problem. Instead, focus on the size of your God.

DAY 3 El Elyon Is the Source

On June 11, 1963, Governor George Wallace and members of his police force stood on the steps of the University of Alabama to prevent two black students from entering. But he had a problem: the federal courts had already decided in the students' favor. Deputy U.S. Attorney General Nicholas Katzenbach and federal marshals arrived with the message "Mr. Governor, step aside."

Wallace vehemently replied that he wasn't going anywhere. That's when the National Guard stepped in, explaining that he could voluntarily leave or they'd forcibly remove him. When those instructions had been made clear, Wallace and his men backed down.

What's interesting is that Governor Wallace held the highest-ranking position in the state of Alabama. So why did he lose the standoff that day? Because the federal courts were higher still, and they overruled Wallace. The higher authority opened the doors not only for two black students but also for an integration movement that spread through college campuses all across the country.

Wallace's story shows that even people who are considered high up must change their course when a higher authority steps in.

As we've seen throughout this study—and especially in Abraham's story—everyone else needs to adjust whenever heaven decides to move. When El Elyon makes a decision, it doesn't matter what anyone's title is here on earth. God will see His decision through, and He will make a way where there seems to be no way from a human point of view.

What are some other historical examples in which God made a way for His will to be done?

When have you been forced to adjust your plans because of God's authority?

As we conclude our exploration of El Elyon today, I'd like to introduce you to a discovery that turned my world upside down decades ago and continues to influence my actions, attitudes, and decisions today. I believe this principle can have the same impact in your life.

The Source and Resources

I mentioned yesterday that Melchizedek was an interesting character in the account of Abraham's efforts to rescue Lot. As a priest and a king, Melchizedek understood the nature of power and the nature of God. He made it clear that Abraham and the 318 men who followed him for 240 miles weren't the ones who'd turned defeat into victory. Someone else was the Source of that victory:

> *[Melchizedek] blessed him and said,*
> *"Blessed be Abram of God Most High,*
> *Possessor of heaven and earth;*
> *And blessed be God Most High,*
> *Who has delivered your*
> *enemies into your hand."*
> **GENESIS 14:19-20**

As we saw yesterday, Abraham and his men weren't the source of the victory and deliverance. But they were *resources* that were involved in that deliverance. The difference between those two ideas is enormous, yet few Christians truly grasp the importance of this truth and live it out on a daily basis.

The spiritual principle of the Source versus the resources came to me when I was in my late 30s as I studied God's Word. When the idea clicked, it was as if a lightbulb turned on in my mind. The principle made a revolutionary difference in my choices, my level of worry, and my planning. Here it is: *God is your Source. Everything else is a resource.*

In other words, God's the only One who can provide something for you. He's the only One who can create something *ex nihilo*—out of nothing—when you have a need. Everything else in this world can be traced back to God, the Source; therefore, everything else in this world is merely a resource.

What's your initial reaction to this spiritual principle?

How would you restate the principle in your own words?

The apostle James wrote about this principle:

> *Do not be deceived, my beloved brethren. Every good thing given and every perfect gift is from above, coming down from the Father of lights, with whom there is no variation or shifting shadow. In the exercise of His will He brought us forth by the word of truth, so that we would be a kind of first fruits among His creatures.*
>
> **JAMES 1:16-18**

How do these verses contribute to your understanding of God as the Source?

In Genesis the kings who were causing problems for Abraham and Lot were kings of earth. Abraham's problem was an earthly situation. Yet because El Elyon is the Source of everything—because He's God Most High—He owns heaven *and* earth. That's why 318 men can look like an army of 30,000 when battling four kings and their armies. El Elyon accompanied them as they remained connected to Him, their Source.

Implications of El Elyon as the Source

This spiritual principle affects the way you interact with everything else in the world that's not God. Specifically, one of the worst things you can do in life is to treat a resource as if it were the Source.

Most of us can rightly judge when we have a need, and we can recognize the provision we'd like to receive for that need. The problem is that we often seek that provision in the wrong places. When we need money, we try to come up with a get-rich-quick scheme. When we're lonely and need companionship, we plow through relationship after relationship trying to fill that void. When we've lost our purpose and need direction in life, we try to smother those feelings of emptiness with entertainment or addictive substances.

The problem with these efforts is that we're trying to receive provision from other resources instead of from the Source. We're trying to convince other created things to create something that can meet our needs. It won't work! We need the Creator. We need to go to the Source—El Elyon—and allow Him to provide what we need from on high.

Why do we so often turn to other resources in an attempt to meet our needs?

When have you tried to receive provision from other created resources? What happened next?

This doesn't mean we should avoid or ignore other created things. It doesn't mean people or possessions can't bless us or have a positive impact in our lives. But whenever that happens, we should recognize that those people or possessions are resources God has used to provide something positive in our lives. He's still the Source.

How has God recently blessed you by providing important resources in your life?

Another way we benefit from understanding the principle of the Source versus resources comes when we experience conflict or affliction. When a resource in your life is messing with you, it doesn't get the last word. God can find another resource through which to bless you and accomplish His plan. As the Source, He has more than one way to accomplish His purposes.

Therefore, nothing and no one can block you from God's plan. No scenario or circumstance can truly stop you—not when you're paired with El Elyon, your Source. As God

Most High, He knows the right path to take if you'll take your eyes off the problems in front of you and turn your eyes toward Him.

> **Confess to El Elyon any areas of your life in which you're seeking resources instead of the Source. Turn over your needs to the Most High God and allow Him to rule over the circumstances of your life.**

DAY 4 Introducing El Shaddai

After decades of serving as a pastor and ministry leader, one thing I've come to understand for certain is that the world is filled with turmoil. The world today is a place of chaos and uncertainty. We don't know what's going to happen from one moment to the next, and it's possible for a new trial or tragedy to sweep aside our goals and routines in an instant.

Today we encounter turmoil in relationships through divorce, abuse, spite, and neglect. We find turmoil in our financial systems, where literally billions of dollars can disappear from our collective pockets in an afternoon. We see turmoil in politics, in celebrity culture, and in education. Even Christians experience turmoil in different aspects of our faith.

> **When have you recently encountered turmoil in your life?**

> **How do you typically respond to uncertain situations and circumstances?**

Younger generations may not use the term *turmoil*. They're more likely to talk about drama in their friends' lives and even in their own situations.

As we move on to our next name of God today, we're going to highlight a family that experienced 25 years of drama while waiting for a particular dream to come true—a specific promise from God. However, even before the fulfillment of that promise, they were blessed by encountering God in a new way and by connecting with the power of His name.

That drama reveals God as El Shaddai—God Almighty.

A Promise Delayed

El Shaddai is one of my favorite names of God. This is a powerful compound connection of El—God—and Shaddai—Almighty or Sufficient. Together as El Shaddai, the name appears 7 times in the Old Testament. God is also referred to as just Shaddai (Almighty) another 41 times.

In Scripture the name El Shaddai is first used during a conversation between God and Abraham (referred to as Abram at the time) in Genesis 17. But to fully appreciate the significance of that conversation, we need to rewind history for a quarter of a century and look at the origins of God's relationship with and promise to His servant Abraham.

Read Genesis 12:1-4. What do these verses teach us about God?

How would you summarize God's promise to Abraham?

Make sure you don't miss this particular detail about Abraham at the time of God's initial promise:

*Abram went, as the LORD had told him, and Lot went with him. **Abram was 75 years old when he left Haran.***
GENESIS 12:4, HCSB, EMPHASIS ADDED

Abraham was 75 years old when God told him He had a special plan and blessing designed for his life. A blessing is God's favor expressed to you in order to bring Him glory. But a blessing never involves *only* what God does for you. He also wants to bless others through you. The blessing must go full circle. It's what God does for you so that the blessing can flow through you to others.

God promised He'd make Abraham "a great nation" (v. 2) but not merely for Abraham's sake. God intended for Abraham's blessing to spread so that "all the peoples on earth" (v. 3, HCSB) would be blessed through him.

What are some ways God has blessed you in recent years?

How have you used those blessings to help others?

When we fast-forward a few years, we see that Abraham had begun to doubt whether God's promise would ever come to fruition. Look at chapter 15:

> Abram said, "Lord GOD, what can You give me, since I am childless and the heir of my house is Eliezer of Damascus?" Abram continued, "Look, You have given me no offspring, so a slave born in my house will be my heir." Now the word of the LORD came to him: "This one will not be your heir; instead, one who comes from your own body will be your heir."

GENESIS 15:2-4, HCSB

Abraham did what many of us try to do today. He tried using logic to create a solution. If God hadn't given Abraham an heir, Abraham would assume that God meant to work through someone in Abraham's household—namely, Eliezer of Damascus. But God was clear: the promise would be fulfilled through Abraham's own son.

Alas, Abraham didn't get the message. He and his wife, Sarai, concocted a new plan to get the ball rolling. They figured that since Sarai had been unable to get pregnant, God must have intended Abraham to conceive the promised son through another woman. And that's exactly the tactic they used next:

> Abram's wife Sarai had not borne any children for him, but she owned an Egyptian slave named Hagar. Sarai said to Abram, "Since the LORD has prevented me from bearing children, go to my slave; perhaps through her I can build a

family." And Abram agreed to what Sarai said.
He slept with Hagar, and she became pregnant.
GENESIS 16:1-2,4, HCSB

What's your initial reaction to this passage?

Why is it so tempting for us to take matters into our own hands rather than relying on God?

Hagar bore a child named Ishmael, who was the father of the Arab peoples. And the Arabs and the Israelites have been in conflict ever since. More importantly, God made it clear that Ishmael wasn't the son He'd promised any more than Eliezer of Damascus (see Gen. 17:18-19). That undoubtedly left Abraham and Sarai feeling old and weary. They waited without an heir, most likely resigned to the conclusion that God had abandoned His promise.

A Promise Fulfilled

That's when we get to Genesis 17. Look at what happened:

When Abram was 99 years old, the LORD appeared to him, saying, "I am God Almighty [El Shaddai]. Live in My presence and be blameless. I will establish My covenant between Me and you, and I will multiply you greatly."
GENESIS 17:1-2, HCSB

Did you catch that age update? Abraham was 99 years old by this point. He'd been waiting on the fulfillment of God's promise for 24 long years. And I'll bet you've learned this lesson by now: waiting isn't easy. Especially when you're waiting for the thing you desire most.

Maybe you can identify with what Abraham and Sarai felt during those long years of waiting. Maybe you feel God has taken too long to meet your needs or to fulfill a promise, such as providing a mate, fixing a marriage, changing a child, solidifying a career, or launching a breakthrough.

What are you waiting for God to provide?

What has God taught you as you've waited for a promise to be fulfilled?

It's in those times of waiting that God reminds us of who He really is. Remember that in Abraham's moment of deepest doubt, God revealed Himself as El Shaddai—God Almighty.

DAY 5 The Comfort of El Shaddai

One day a man went fishing with his friend. Before long the friend caught a fairly large fish. He quickly took the fish off his hook and threw it back in the water. A few minutes passed, and then the friend caught another huge fish. Once again, he took it off the hook and threw it back in the water.

At this point the man assumed his friend was fishing for sport, not for food. But then his friend caught a smaller fish and kept it, placing it in a bucket near the water's edge. "I don't understand," the man said. "Why did you throw the big ones back but keep that small one?"

His friend answered, "My frying pan is only 10 inches wide."

If you're looking at life based on what you can handle—what you can produce and what you have the capacity to bring about—then you're no doubt throwing back what God wants to do in and through you to bring about blessings for others. You're settling for the little you can accomplish on your own rather than the miracle of El Shaddai.

How do you know when it's time to trust God with something rather than continuing your efforts to succeed?

Today we're going to look deeper into the implications of knowing El Shaddai—God Almighty. As we do, be sure to keep this principle in mind: never look at the size of your frying pan, because it will always be too small. Instead, look at the size of your God and remember His name.

The Meaning of El Shaddai

I've already told you that El Shaddai means God Almighty. But digging a little deeper into the roots of that name can be both interesting and informative, especially in connection with the story of Abraham and Sarah.

You may remember that El is the singular form of Elohim, which means the Strong Creator God. The term Shaddai is a little more obscure. It comes from the root word *shad,* which is literally translated *breast.* The prophet Isaiah used that same word picture in passages like these:

> *You will also suck the milk of nations*
> *And suck the breast [shad] of kings;*
> *Then you will know that I, the*
> *LORD, am your Savior*
> *And your Redeemer, the*
> *Mighty One of Jacob.*
> ISAIAH 60:16

> *Be joyful with Jerusalem and rejoice*
> *for her, all you who love her;*
> *Be exceedingly glad with her, all*
> *you who mourn over her,*
> *That you may nurse and be satisfied with*
> *her comforting breasts [shad],*
> *That you may suck and be delighted*
> *with her bountiful bosom.*
> ISAIAH 66:10-11

What's your initial reaction to these verses?

Both of these passages use the word *shad* to signify the supply of nourishment. When a woman nurses her baby, she supplies what the child needs to live. Therefore, when the name El Shaddai is understood in connection with its root meaning, it presents the image of God supplying the nourishment needed to sustain life.

Abraham and Sarah's problem was that they couldn't produce life. Sarah was barren and couldn't give birth to children. Abraham and Sarah didn't understand how God's promise could possibly be fulfilled, since it was entirely contingent on Sarah's having a baby.

Maybe you've felt the same way. Have you ever been dragged down by your own inability to produce what God has promised in your life? Do you wonder whether even God can work things out because of how little you have to offer?

When have you been confronted by the inability to accomplish the goals God has set for your life?

When you find yourself in those kinds of situations, remember El Shaddai is the God who can create something from nothing. He did it in Genesis 1 as Elohim—the strong Creator. The Book of Hebrews makes it clear:

> *By faith we understand that the worlds were prepared by the word of God, so that what is seen was not made out of things which are visible.*
> **HEBREWS 11:3**

Not only can God create life from nothing as Elohim, but He can also sustain that life through His power as El Shaddai—God Almighty. Let me be clear: He does that through *His* power. That means you don't have to figure things out through *your* power. God doesn't need your help, just as He didn't need Abraham and Sarah's attempt to carry out His plan by turning to Hagar for conception.

How has God created something from nothing in your life?

God is both the Creator and the Sustainer of life, and He loves to manifest Himself in the midst of the impossible. That's just one implication of the name El Shaddai in our lives today. There are others.

Implications of the Name El Shaddai

When we, as followers of Christ, understand the meaning and relevance of the name El Shaddai, we should be driven to spend more time in God's presence. That's the message at the beginning of one of my favorite psalms:

> *He who dwells in the shelter of*
> *the Most High [El Elyon]*
> *Will abide in the shadow of*
> *the Almighty [Shaddai].*
> *I will say to the LORD [Jehovah],*
>   *"My refuge and my fortress,*
> *My God [Elohim], in whom I trust!"*
> **PSALM 91:1-2**

Can you see why I love that psalm? Four names of God in just two verses. The psalmist says if we dwell where God dwells—"in the shelter of the Most High" (v. 1)—He will do more in our lives. Right after revealing His name as El Shaddai, God told Abraham to "walk before Me" (Gen. 17:1). In the same way, God wants you to walk before Him and dwell in His presence at all times.

Jesus put it this way:

> *I am the vine, you are the branches; he who*
> *abides in Me and I in him, he bears much fruit,*
> *for apart from Me you can do nothing.*
> **JOHN 15:5**

What steps do you take to spend time in God's presence?

How have you benefited from time spent abiding with Him?

Another implication of El Shaddai in our lives is that the name should spur us to hope. We worship God Almighty; therefore, we can hope for the best and choose to praise God, even in the darkest situations.

Abraham was in a seemingly hopeless situation. He was a 99-year-old man who deeply desired to father a child. Everything in the world said Abraham should turn his back on God's promise. Instead, he chose to hope:

> *In hope against hope [Abraham] believed, so that he might become a father of many nations according to that which had been spoken.*
>
> **ROMANS 4:18**

Abraham ultimately saw the fruit of his hope and belief through the birth of his son, Isaac (see Gen. 21:1-7).

For what situation in your life do you need to place more hope in El Shaddai?

You will also see the fruit of your belief when you choose to hope in God. Put your hope in El Shaddai today. He knows you. He loves you. And He will sustain you when you trust Him to fulfill His promises in you and through you.

Spend time today in the shadow of God Almighty, El Shaddai. Pray about any specific promise He's given you. Commit your life to Him and ask Him to bring about His purposes in and through you according to His timing and His plan.

CHAPTER 6

IMMANUEL

INTRODUCTION A Familiar Power

I don't know who coined the phrase "Familiarity breeds contempt," but he or she was right on. The more we're exposed to something, the more we become dissatisfied or disillusioned with it. We can even get to the point that we feel sick of what we once enjoyed or appreciated.

This usually happens in mundane ways. For example, if you eat pancakes for breakfast day after day, you may begin to feel your appreciation for pancakes waning. You may begin to crave other items—cereal, eggs, bacon, or toast. If you continue dining on pancakes without a break, they may become a despised food choice rather than a preferred menu item.

The same principle can cause us to grow tired of television shows, restaurants, clothes, and hobbies. Again, most of these evolving preferences are harmless.

In other instances, however, familiarity can lead us to dismiss something vital— something critical to our lives and the lives of others. For example, our constant overexposure to the Christmas holiday has led many families, even Christian families, to disregard the revolutionary nature of the event at its core. We can become so accustomed to stockings and shopping lists that we ignore the shocking detail of God's taking the form of a human baby and manifesting Himself on earth.

But that's not the worst of it. I'm convinced that many people in the Christian community have become overly familiar with the Person at the heart of the Christmas story—at the heart of everything. I'm talking about Jesus. I'm talking about Immanuel—God with Us.

As we'll see this week, the name of Jesus is filled with deep meaning and abundant power. But we'll never plumb the depths of that name if we allow its familiarity to produce apathy or contempt in our hearts.

So this week let's take a fresh look at Immanuel—our Savior, Jesus—whose name is the fulfillment of all names and is inferior to none.

DAY 1 Introducing Immanuel

If you came over to my house around Christmastime, you'd notice a number of fairly large gift boxes sitting outside the front door of our home. These gloriously decorated boxes make an appearance each year, embodying all the color, glitter, and shine associated with the most materialistic holiday of the year.

There's only one problem: the boxes are empty. They're nothing more than decorations. If someone stole them from our house while we were gone, they'd have some well-wrapped boxes and nothing more.

What are some of your favorite traditions of the Christmas season?

Our decorative Christmas boxes represent all the fanfare of Christmas but none of the meaning. They have all the external trappings of the holiday, but they have no value inside.

Sadly, those decorative packages are like many Christians today. I know because I've had a lot of experience with those kinds of Christians. They dress to the nines for church and carry a Bible. They can sometimes quote a few Bible verses, and they may even teach Sunday School or lead a small group.

But if we unwrapped the fancy bow and peeled away the paper from these Christians' lives, we wouldn't find anything of value inside. Specifically, we wouldn't find the abundant life of Jesus Christ.

And Jesus makes all the difference.

How does our culture regard and define Jesus Christ today?

Our culture goes out of its way to define Jesus in ways that are contrary to His true identity revealed in Scripture. But as we'll see this week, Jesus is the very essence of God, who came to take away the sins of the world and reveal the Father to us in the flesh. He's Immanuel—God with Us.

Prophesying the Savior

Immanuel is the final name of God we'll explore together in this study. That's intentional, because Immanuel embodies and fulfills all the other names we've examined so far. Jesus is the final and authoritative revelation of God's character.

For that reason it's appropriate that we start our exploration of Jesus' name in the Old Testament rather than the New Testament. After all, much of the old covenant serves as a backdrop for and a foreshadowing of the new covenant established by Christ.

Where have you seen Jesus foreshadowed or referenced in the Old Testament?

The first mention of Immanuel in God's Word comes in the Book of Isaiah. At the time Isaiah prophesied, the nation of Judah's international situation was dangerous. Enemies all around had gathered strength, and the king, Ahaz, was nervous about the future for himself and for his people. Therefore, God sent Isaiah to comfort Ahaz with an interesting message:

The LORD spoke again to Ahaz, saying, "Ask a sign for yourself from the LORD your God; make it deep as Sheol or high as heaven." But Ahaz said, "I will not ask, nor will I test the LORD!" Then he said, "Listen now, O house of David! Is it too slight a thing for you to try the patience of men, that you will try the patience of my God as well?"

ISAIAH 7:10-13

Here's a piece of advice: if God invites you to ask Him for something, take Him up on it. Ahaz wasn't sure whether he should impose on God. He thought he was being pious by refusing God's request for a sign, but all he really did was try God's patience.

Look at what God said next:

> *Therefore the Lord Himself will give you a sign:*
> *Behold, a virgin will be with child and bear a*
> *son, and she will call His name Immanuel.*
>
> **ISAIAH 7:14**

I like the phrase "Therefore the Lord Himself will give you a sign." Ahaz refused to ask for a sign, but God's news was so good that He couldn't keep it to Himself. He wanted to bless His people with a message of hope.

Interestingly, this was a multilayered message. On one level God told Ahaz that in just a few years—in the time it would take for a new child to be born and grow toward maturity (see v. 16)—his enemies would no longer be a threat.

But on another level God's message was also a long-term prophecy of the greater hope that was coming in the form of the Messiah, Jesus Christ. We know this because of the divine message that was delivered several hundred years later to Joseph, Jesus' earthly father, after he learned Mary was pregnant:

> *"Joseph, son of David, do not be afraid to take Mary as*
> *your wife; for the Child who has been conceived in her is of*
> *the Holy Spirit. She will bear a Son; and you shall call His*
> *name Jesus, for He will save His people from their sins."*
> *Now all this took place to fulfill what was spoken by the*
> *Lord through the prophet: "Behold, the virgin shall be with*
> *child and shall bear a Son, and they shall call His name*
> *Immanuel," which translated means, "God with us."*
>
> **MATTHEW 1:20-23**

What new information did the angel provide about Jesus?

Ancestors of Christ

Two men in the Old Testament are connected to Jesus and His name Immanuel. The first is Joshua.

When the angel Gabriel visited Mary to foretell the birth
of the Messiah, he instructed her to name the baby Jesus,
because that name meant He'd save His people from their
sins (see Luke 1:31-32). Jesus is the New Testament equivalent
of the Old Testament name Joshua, which means *salvation*.

Joshua and Jesus. The two names create an interesting
link, given that Joshua was a primary agent in rescuing
God's chosen people from slavery in Egypt and delivering
them to the promised land.

**Read Joshua 1:1-9. What similarities do you see between
Joshua and Jesus in these verses?**

**What differences do you notice, based on God's
instructions to Joshua?**

The other Old Testament character who bears a strong link
with Immanuel is David, a former shepherd who rose to
become the king of Israel and was described as a man after
God's own heart (see 1 Sam. 13:14). God made the following
covenant with David after he was firmly established as king:

*When your days are complete and you lie down with
your fathers, I will raise up your descendant after you,
who will come forth from you, and I will establish his
kingdom. He shall build a house for My name, and
I will establish the throne of his kingdom forever.*

2 SAMUEL 7:12-13

How do these verses point to Jesus?

Why do I bring up these Old Testament characters in a lesson
about Jesus? Because it's important for us to remember that
God had established the promise of Immanuel—the promise of
God with Us—thousands of years before Jesus arrived on earth.

Long before Mary, the shepherds, and the wise men,
God had planned to reveal Himself in a new way to His

people. He'd planned to reveal Himself as Savior and rescue us from our sins. He'd planned to establish a new kingdom forever so that we could always know and experience Immanuel—God with Us.

How have you experienced Jesus as Savior?

DAY 2 God with Us

Who is Jesus? You may think that's an easy question to answer, and in some ways it is. But that question has also been the source of conflict and strife for centuries throughout the history of the church. It's also a question that keeps being reasked and reanswered each generation as people discover Him and His story for the first time.

How would you answer the question, Who is Jesus?

The nature of Christ has been one of the primary sources of controversies connected with Jesus over the centuries. Is He a divine Being? Is He a created being? Is He God, or was He merely a man?

The most famous explosion surrounding these questions came between A.D. 300 and 400, when the church was confronted with a popular (but heretical) doctrine called Arianism. To make a long story short, Arius was a theologian who believed Jesus was the most important part of God's creation but still a created being. In other words, Arius believed Jesus was more than a regular human being but less than God.

Arius's famous statement on the matter was this: "There was a time when the Son was not."[1]

Fortunately, the church rejected the doctrine of Arianism, although it took a while. Led by an African theologian named Athanasius, the church proclaimed Jesus to be both fully divine and fully human at the Council of Nicea in A.D. 325 and then reaffirmed that understanding at the Council of Constantinople in 381.

What are false messages our culture communicates about Jesus?

Of course, everyone could have saved themselves a lot of time, effort, and drama if they'd simply focused more on the power of Jesus' name Immanuel. That one name told them everything they needed to know about Jesus—God with Us.

Jesus Is God

When the angel spoke to Mary about Jesus' birth, he said, "You will conceive in your womb and bear a son, and you shall name Him Jesus" (Luke 1:31). We need to understand that the essence of this passage and of the historical event it records isn't simply the birth of a baby. The essence is that God *became* a baby. God somehow condensed His majesty and power and manifested Himself inside a young woman's womb.

Interestingly, this idea had been communicated centuries earlier in another prophecy from the Book of Isaiah:

> *A child will be born to us, a*
> *son will be given to us;*
> *And the government will*
> *rest on His shoulders;*
> *And His name will be called*
> *Wonderful Counselor, Mighty God,*
> *Eternal Father, Prince of Peace.*
> ISAIAH 9:6

What do these verses teach us about Jesus?

Notice that the child is "born," but the Son is "given." That's because the Son existed before the child was born. The virgin gave birth to a child, but the Son existed before the virgin even became pregnant—before she was even born!

Read the following passages of Scripture. Record how each contributes to the doctrine that Jesus is fully God.

Colossians 1:15-20

Hebrews 1:1-3

Jesus Himself declared His divinity on a number of occasions. In fact, the main reason the Pharisees and religious leaders believed Jesus deserved to die was that He'd declared Himself to be equal with God (see Matt. 26:59-64). On that same night Jesus had a revealing conversation with His disciple Philip:

> Philip said to Him, "Lord, show us the Father, and it is enough for us." Jesus said to him, "Have I been so long with you, and yet you have not come to know Me, Philip? He who has seen Me has seen the Father; how can you say, 'Show us the Father'? Do you not believe that I am in the Father, and the Father is in Me? The words that I say to you I do not speak on My own initiative, but the Father abiding in Me does His works."
>
> **JOHN 14:8-10**

How do Jesus' words help you understand His nature?

Philip had been Jesus' disciple for three years, and yet he still didn't have a full picture of who Jesus is. Sadly, the same can be true of us when we don't grasp the full meaning of Immanuel—God with Us.

Jesus Is God with Us

One of my favorite explorations of Jesus' nature and character comes from the opening of John's Gospel. It's a lovely passage that condenses the core elements of Jesus' nature and mission into a memorable mix of imagery and prose.

Look at the way it starts:

*In the beginning was the Word, and the Word
was with God, and the Word was God. He was
in the beginning with God. All things came into
being through Him, and apart from Him nothing
came into being that has come into being.*

JOHN 1:1-3

The Word John wrote about was Immanuel—God with Us.
Jesus is the very representation and likeness of God. He
was "with God" (v. 1) in the beginning, not because He was
just hanging around and not because God created Him first.
Rather, Jesus "was God" (v. 1).

But John didn't stop there:

*The Word became flesh, and dwelt among us, and
we saw His glory, glory as of the only begotten
from the Father, full of grace and truth.*

JOHN 1:14

Jesus walked among us. He was flesh, bones, sinews, and
blood, and yet He was also perfectly divine. At one moment
He was hungry because of His human nature, and in the
next moment He fed five thousand men with a few loaves
and fish because of His divine nature. He could be thirsty
because He was fully human, but He could also walk on
water because He was fully God.

In a similar way, Jesus agonized on a Roman cross and
died because He was fully human. He possessed a physical
body, and that body lost the spark of life. And yet Jesus rose
from the grave three days later because He was fully God—
the Creator of all bodies and all things.

**Why is understanding Jesus' nature important to the way
you live?**

You and I need to realize that without Immanuel—without Jesus—we have no chance of understanding God. John made that clear a few verses later:

No one has seen God at any time; the only begotten God who is in the bosom of the Father, He has explained Him.

JOHN 1:18

What steps have you taken to connect with Jesus and learn more about Him?

How have you experienced Jesus as God with Us?

How does God make Himself known? Through Immanuel—God with Us. Therefore, to understand and know Jesus is to understand and know God.

DAY 3 The Wonder of His Name

When you share your name with most people, you use the form of your name that's most common and comfortable to you. For example, most people use their first and last names together. That's why I'm most often introduced to other people as Tony Evans.

Even so, I have other names I don't use as often but are still connected to me, and so do you. For example, although I typically use the name Tony when I introduce myself, that's not my actual name. My full given name is Anthony.

Most people in today's culture also have a middle name in addition to their first and last names. My middle name is Tyrone, but I rarely use it. It's rare that you'd hear me say, "Hi. I'm Anthony Tyrone Evans." Shorter is simpler.

There are also a number of different titles that have become attached to my name over the years. For example, people call me Dr. Tony Evans when they want to recognize my achievements in higher education. Or people call me Pastor Evans when referring to my vocation and calling in life.

What are the different names people use to describe you?

In addition to Immanuel, Jesus also has other names. These aren't literal names you'd use in conversation; rather, they're descriptive names that give us insight into His character and mission. We can find four of these names by looking at this prophecy from the Book of Isaiah:

> *A child will be born to us, a*
> *son will be given to us;*
> *And the government will*
> *rest on His shoulders;*
> *And His name will be called*
> *Wonderful Counselor, Mighty God,*
> *Eternal Father, Prince of Peace.*
> ISAIAH 9:6

Which of the previous names of Jesus resonates with you most? Explain your response.

Let's explore each of these names of Jesus to gain a better understanding of and appreciation for Immanuel—God with Us.

Wonderful Counselor

When members of our congregation come to me for counseling, the quality of advice they receive depends on the kind of day I'm having. People often come expecting a pearl of wisdom that will instantly solve their problems and immediately put their lives in order. Unfortunately, I'm only human. I can't hit the bulls-eye 100 percent of the time, regardless of how hard I try. My personal resources and experiences are limited.

That's what makes Jesus the Wonderful Counselor. His perspective is infinite, and His resources are unlimited. He's God, so He brings every possible source of knowledge and understanding to the table on our behalf.

At the same time, He has an intimate understanding of the kinds of trouble we often face:

131

Since we have a great high priest who has passed through the heavens, Jesus the Son of God, let us hold fast our confession. For we do not have a high priest who cannot sympathize with our weaknesses, but One who has been tempted in all things as we are, yet without sin. Therefore let us draw near with confidence to the throne of grace, so that we may receive mercy and find grace to help in time of need.

HEBREWS 4:14-16

Why is it important that Jesus can sympathize with our weaknesses and areas of struggle (see v. 15)?

Why is it important to remember that Jesus is "without sin" (v. 15)?

Jesus is God, yet He also spent a lifetime on earth enduring the same kinds of trials and temptations we face. Therefore, who could be better qualified to offer us guidance and direction?

What steps can you take to maximize Jesus' role as Counselor in your life?

Mighty God

Jesus never fails. He's faithful to do all for us He's promised. How can we be sure? Because of the testimony of His mighty acts, both in creation and in the many miracles He performed on earth.

Read the following passages and record ways they support Scripture's claim that Jesus is mighty (see Isa. 9:6).

Matthew 8:23-27

Mark 6:33-44

John 11:30-46

The same hands that formed the mountains, oceans, and the sky are strong enough to defeat any enemy yet gentle enough to comfort any heart. Might is more than strength. Might is the ability to use strength strategically for the good of others. Jesus—God with Us—embodies might in its most perfect form.

Where do you currently need Jesus' might in your life?

Everlasting Father

Have you ever pondered where God came from? Here's some free advice: don't waste your time. God didn't come from anywhere, because He's always existed. Concepts like everywhere and everything have their source in Him.

According to the Book of Revelation, the same is true of Jesus. A lot of people get confused by Revelation, but it's a lot clearer if we remember that the first verse labels the entire text as "the Revelation of Jesus Christ" (Rev. 1:1). The entire Book of Revelation is centered on Christ, including this statement:

"I am the Alpha and the Omega," says the Lord God, "who is and who was and who is to come, the Almighty."
REVELATION 1:8

God has transcended time and space to make Himself known through the Person of Jesus. And He will continue to do so forever.

Why is it important to understand that Jesus is eternal?

How does Jesus' eternal nature affect your life as His disciple?

Prince of Peace

Humanity desperately wants peace. Rulers sit around tables and negotiate for peace. They pay high prices and make substantial compromises for peace. If that fails, they go to war in order to achieve peace.

But the truth is that few of us understand what peace actually is. Many of us wouldn't recognize it if we saw it, because we're so frequently unsettled within. Because we don't have internal peace, it's virtually impossible for us to work for and experience peace in the world.

Jesus provides an alternative to this lifelong struggle. He alone can grant us the peace that comes through the forgiveness of sin and the confident purpose we achieve when following Him. The apostle Paul understood that kind of peace:

Not that I speak from want, for I have learned to be content in whatever circumstances I am. I know how to get along with humble means, and I also know how to live in prosperity; in any and every circumstance I have learned the secret of being filled and going hungry, both of having abundance and suffering need. I can do all things through Him who strengthens me.

PHILIPPIANS 4:11-13

During which seasons of your life have you felt content?

How can you seek contentment and peace through your relationship with Jesus?

Most of us believe peace is the absence of conflict. Thankfully, Jesus offers much more. He promises the kind of peace that transcends our circumstances and invades the natural conflicts that arise in a sinful world. It's easy to be at peace when all's well. But Jesus, the perfect Prince of Peace, promises us a peace that "surpasses all comprehension" (Phil. 4:7).

Praise Jesus today as Wonderful Counselor, Mighty God, Everlasting Father, and Prince of Peace. What has Jesus done for you in these roles for which you'd like to praise Him?

DAY 4 The Name of Salvation

Have you ever thought about the different definitions of the word *save*? A quick look at the dictionary turns up quite a few:

- To rescue from danger or possible harm, injury, or loss: *to save someone from drowning.*
- To keep safe, intact, or unhurt; safeguard; preserve: *God save the king.*
- To keep from being lost: *to save the game.*
- To avoid the spending, consumption, or waste of: *to save fuel.*
- To keep, as for reuse: *to save leftovers for tomorrow's dinner.*[2]

The reason I bring up the word *save* is that we talk a lot about the doctrine of salvation in the church today. As Christians, we proclaim that only Jesus saves, and we assert that those who haven't experienced a personal relationship with Him need to be saved.

But what exactly do we mean by that term? By its nature, the term *save* raises two important questions we need to answer if we want others to understand what we mean:

1. What are we saved from?
2. What are we saved to?

How do you answer those questions?

What other questions would you like answered about the meaning and process of salvation?

My goal today is to answer those questions by exploring Jesus' mission on earth and what that mission means for us.

If you're already a follower of Christ and have a good understanding of what it means to be saved, you may be tempted to skip this material. I strongly encourage you to resist that temptation. Yes, we're going to explore the gospel, but I encourage you to do so with fresh eyes. Remember what you've learned about the power of God's names, and let that new information influence the way you see the saving work of Jesus Christ.

How confident do you feel about your understanding of what it means to be saved by Jesus Christ?

1	2	3	4	5	6	7	8	9	10

Not confident   **Fully confident**

If you're not a follower of Jesus or if you don't fully understand what it means to be saved by Him, please read on. You'll discover another layer of meaning in the power of God's names, especially in the name Immanuel—God with Us.

We're Saved from Sin

To answer the question "What are we saved from?" let's look at the message Joseph received in a dream after learning his fiancée was pregnant:

*Joseph, son of David, do not be afraid to take Mary as your wife; for the Child who has been conceived in her is of the Holy Spirit. She will bear a Son; and you shall call His name Jesus, **for He will save His people from their sins.***
MATTHEW 1:20-21, EMPHASIS ADDED

What ideas or images come to mind when you hear the word *sin*?

Jesus came to save us from our sins. Specifically, He came to provide a way for our sins to be legally forgiven and for us to be released from the punishment we deserve because of our sins. It's a good thing, because that punishment is death:

> *The wages of sin is death, but the free gift of*
> *God is eternal life in Christ Jesus our Lord.*
> **ROMANS 6:23**

This connection between sin and death isn't a new arrangement. It goes all the way back to the beginning.

Read Genesis 3:1-7. How do these verses contribute to your understanding of sin?

When Adam and Eve chose to violate God's command and rebel against His authority, they introduced corruption into the world God had made for them—a world that had been perfect prior to that rebellion. This corruption is what we commonly refer to as sin. When Adam and Eve came in contact with that corruption, it immediately began the deterioration of their physical bodies. Ultimately, their sin led to their deaths. Sadly, their sin corrupted not only themselves but also every human being who came after them, including you and me.

But physical death wasn't the only consequence of sin. Because God is perfect, anything sinful is automatically excluded from His presence. Sin creates a separation between us and God in the same way light is automatically separated from darkness. Throughout the centuries theologians have referred to this separation as the second death or spiritual death. Ultimately, this spiritual death leads to eternal separation from God, which is the reality known as hell.

How does our society interpret the concept of hell?

How would you summarize your beliefs about heaven and hell?

Thankfully, that's not the end of the story. As we've said this week, God chose to take the form of a man. He came to earth as Immanuel—God with Us—and He lived among us for decades as a man named Jesus. In the end Jesus allowed Himself to be killed on a cross to solve the problem of sin once and for all.

Because He's God, Jesus was able to absorb all the punishment for sin—the punishment of eternal separation from God that we were destined to experience (see John 19:16-30). Having taken that punishment away, Jesus defeated the power of death by rising from the grave on the third day (see 20:1-18). His resurrection proved that He's God, and because of that proof, we as Christians have a sure hope of joining Him in eternal life.

These concepts are summarized in what may be the most famous Scripture passage of all:

God so loved the world, that He gave His only begotten Son, that whoever believes in Him shall not perish, but have eternal life. For God did not send the Son into the world to judge the world, but that the world might be saved through Him.

JOHN 3:16-17

We're Saved into His Kingdom

Let's move on to the second important question: "What are we saved to?" That question was answered by another angelic proclamation before Jesus' birth—this time to Jesus' mother, Mary:

*Behold, you will conceive in your womb and bear a son, and you shall name Him Jesus. He will be great and will be called the Son of the Most High; and the Lord God will give Him the throne of His father David; and He will reign over the house of Jacob forever, and **His kingdom will have no end.***

LUKE 1:31-33, EMPHASIS ADDED

A central truth of the Christian faith is that life involves more than the physical world. There's also a spiritual realm—a spiritual kingdom—in which God is the King. When we say

Immanuel is God with Us, we mean Jesus left the spiritual realm and physically manifested Himself in our world.

When we experience salvation, then, we enter God's spiritual kingdom for all eternity. We live as members of that kingdom here on earth, and we work in partnership with God to advance the mission and purpose of His kingdom so that others can benefit as well. Then, when our bodies deteriorate and we experience physical death, we fully enter God's kingdom as spiritual beings. This is heaven:

We know that if the earthly tent which is our house is torn down, we have a building from God, a house not made with hands, eternal in the heavens. For indeed in this house we groan, longing to be clothed with our dwelling from heaven.
2 CORINTHIANS 5:1-2

What questions do you still have about the doctrine and process of salvation?

Where can you go to find answers to those questions?

The doctrine of salvation is intimately connected with the power of God's name Immanuel. Because He's God with Us, He can save us from our sins and bring us into His kingdom of eternal life. Our response to that invitation is the most important decision we'll ever make.

DAY 5 The Name Above All Names

We live in a culture of celebrities. They're all around us. We hold these people in high regard because of their ability to act, sing, play sports, and so on. We esteem these individuals for their status and significance.

Unfortunately for those who've reached the pinnacle of popularity, celebrity status can be a tenuous prize. Our society is notorious for losing interest in celebrities and casting them aside. This is partly due to our fickle nature, but it's also due to the reality that skills, talents, and even notoriety eventually decline. When enough time passes, almost everyone becomes forgotten.

Jesus stands in contrast to every other celebrity in the history of the world. He's the most important and most influential person who ever lived. In fact, He's the most famous person in all recorded history, and that will never change.

It's remarkable when you think about it. Jesus never wrote a song, yet more songs have been written about Him than any other person who ever lived. Jesus never wrote a book, yet the Book written about Him, the Bible, has outsold every other book. Jesus never traveled more than three hundred miles from the place of His birth, yet people in every corner of the earth recognize His name.

Jesus Christ is the key to all human history, and He's the key to your eternal future. He's God!

What have you learned about Jesus this week?

As we conclude our exploration of Immanuel and our entire study together, I'd like to show you two more truths about Jesus that can help you understand and experience the power of His name in your life.

Jesus Fulfills God's Names

I've mentioned that the entire scope of the Old Testament Scriptures serves as a backdrop for Jesus and His entrance into the world. In addition, Jesus fulfills every one of God's names, including the ones we've explored in this study:

ELOHIM—THE CREATOR GOD: "By Him all things were created, both in the heavens and on earth, visible and invisible, whether thrones or dominions or rulers or authorities—all things have been created through Him and for Him" (Col. 1:16).

JEHOVAH—THE RELATIONAL GOD: "The glory which You have given Me I have given to them, that they may be one, just as We are one; I in them and You in Me, that they may be perfected in unity, so that the world may know that You sent Me, and loved them, even as You have loved Me" (John 17:22-23).

ADONAI—THE GOD WHO RULES: "Why do you call Me, 'Lord, Lord,' and do not do what I say?" (Luke 6:46).

JEHOVAH NISSI—THE LORD MY BANNER: "These things I have spoken to you, so that in Me you may have peace. In the world you have tribulation, but take courage; I have overcome the world" (John 16:33).

JEHOVAH TSABA—THE LORD OUR WARRIOR: "I saw heaven opened, and behold, a white horse, and He who sat on it is called Faithful and True, and in righteousness He judges and wages war" (Rev. 19:11).

JEHOVAH ROHI—THE LORD MY SHEPHERD: "I am the good shepherd, and I know My own and My own know Me. My sheep hear My voice, and I know them, and they follow Me; and I give eternal life to them, and they will never perish; and no one will snatch them out of My hand" (John 10:14,27-28).

JEHOVAH JIREH—THE LORD OUR PROVIDER: "Jesus said to them, 'I am the bread of life; he who comes to Me will not hunger, and he who believes in Me will never thirst' " (John 6:35).

EL ELYON—THE MOST HIGH GOD: "Every created thing which is in heaven and on the earth and under the earth and on the sea, and all things in them, I heard saying, 'To Him who sits on the throne, and to the Lamb, be blessing and honor and glory and dominion forever and ever' " (Rev. 5:13).

EL SHADDAI—GOD ALMIGHTY: " 'I am the Alpha and the Omega,' says the Lord God, 'who is and who was and who is to come, the Almighty' " (Rev. 1:8).

How does the previous list influence your perception of Jesus?

Why is it important to understand that Jesus fulfills all the other names of God?

Jesus' Name Is Superior

I love the way Paul summarized Jesus' actions and attitudes in Philippians 2:

> *Have this attitude in yourselves which was also in Christ Jesus, who, although He existed in the form of God, did not regard equality with God a thing to be grasped, but emptied Himself, taking the form of a bond-servant, and being made in the likeness of men. Being found in appearance as a man, He humbled Himself by becoming obedient to the point of death, even death on a cross.*
>
> **PHILIPPIANS 2:5-8**

The good news of Jesus Christ is that no matter how low you go, He knows what you're feeling. That's because He came and lived as a servant, humble and lowly. He came with a passion and a purpose: to bring salvation to humanity by taking on the sins of the world. But to accomplish that, He had to humble Himself.

How does it make you feel to know that Jesus humbled Himself for your benefit?

However, Jesus hasn't remained lowly. Because of His incredible sacrifice, He's been given a name superior to all other names:

> *For this reason also, God highly exalted Him, and bestowed on Him the name which is above every name, so that at the name of Jesus every knee will bow, of those who are in heaven and on earth and under the earth, and that every tongue will confess that Jesus Christ is Lord, to the glory of God the Father.*
>
> **PHILIPPIANS 2:9-11**

One day every knee will bow at Jesus' name. One day every tongue will confess that He's Lord—that He's Elohim, Jehovah, and all the others. In Greek the name Jesus means Savior, Salvation, or Deliverer. Of all the names of God, the name of Jesus opens the floodgates of His greatest power, both now and forevermore.

How will you respond to the power of Jesus' name?

I think it's appropriate to end this study with the same challenge I used to start it: don't be satisfied with knowing about Jesus. You've spent weeks studying a lot of specific names for God, and you've learned a lot of information about the power of those names.

But don't stop there, especially with Jesus—Immanuel. Knowing *about* Jesus won't do you much good, but knowing Him intimately and personally will radically change your life. And in order to truly know Jesus, you must experience Him personally. Abide with Him. Hang out in His presence. Discover what brings Him pleasure and what He wants to do in you, for you, and through you.

Then you'll truly encounter and begin to understand the power of God's names.

What will you do to know Jesus more intimately?

Praise Jesus today as the Name above all names. Select the name of God that speaks to you most clearly today and praise Jesus as the fulfillment of that name.

1. Philip Schaff, *Nicene and Post-Nicene Fathers Series 2, Volume 2* [online, cited 21 November 2013]. Available from the Internet: www.ccel.org/ccel/schaff/npnf202.
2. "Save," Dictionary.com [online, cited 21 November 2013]. Available from the Internet: http://dictionary.reference.com.